The Garden of God

TITLES IN THE SERIES

The Garden of God

A Theological Cosmology

Alejandro Garcia-Rivera

FORTRESS PRESS
MINNEAPOLIS

THE GARDEN OF GOD
A Theological Cosmology

Cover image: *Girasole*, Arthur Poulin, O.S.B. Cam. Used with permission.

Library of Congress Cataloging-in-Publication Data

Garcia-Rivera, Alex.
The garden of God: a theological cosmology / Alejandro Garcia-Rivera.
    p. cm.
ISBN 978-0-8006-6358-2 (alk. paper)
1. Biblical cosmology. 2. Cosmogony. I. Title.
BS651.G253 2009
231.7—dc22
                    2009017616

Manufactured in the U.S.A.

Contents

Preface

My work on *The Garden of God* actually began about thirty years ago. I was a young physicist working for Boeing at their home plant in Seattle. For the most part, I did fairly routine work investigating mechanical problems occurring in a variety of Boeing's jets. One day, however, I was assigned to a project shrouded in secrecy. All I saw of the project was a computer monitor inside a trailer. That computer, however, had a large cable that went out from the trailer and traveled almost a mile to a hangar at the end of the field, ominously guarded by what looked to be Air Force servicemen with guns.

As I entered the trailer the first time, I was puzzled as to why I had been given this assignment. I had an entry-level job, after all. Nonetheless, I stood as I booted up the computer. In front of me flashed four letters that quietly entered my consciousness but soon began screaming in alarm—A L C M. It suddenly hit me. This was the Air Launch Cruise Missile project I had heard so much about! The sudden realization led me to a powerful experience unlike any I have ever had before and, after all these years, to writing this book.

I fell into a kind of waking dream, a mystical-like experience. The black tarmac outside the trailer began to envelop all of Boeing field and I could see, smell, and hear the flame, smoke, and roar of a terrible conflagration. I knew as a physicist the destructiveness and toxicity of nuclear forces. I had gone into science for my love of the beauty of nature. Now I was seeing, feeling the dark side. After being overwhelmed by this vision of hell, the consequences of continuing to work on this project began to sink in. I would be helping bring hell to earth. I sat down heavily on my chair and asked myself the question, Do I really want my life to be marked by using my skill, my knowledge, and my will to bring about the possibility of such a conflagration? How many would die because of what I do here today? What sort of science is this that can bring hell to earth?

These questions still linger within me. I am now a theologian, but I have struggled with integrating that experience into my theology. Mystical visions are supposed to be moments of great ecstasy. What does one do with a mystical vision of hell? I found an answer in the works of the great Jesuit theologian Teilhard de Chardin. Theology, he saw, was intrinsically cosmic. Salvation for the human has high stakes. It not only involves the human but the entire universe. The universe and humanity are connected because the human is a phenomenon in the universe. We were not created outside of the universe and then put into it but are of the universe and for the universe. Indeed, in a more radical way than any other creature, the universe is meant to be home to the human. Thus part of the human phenomenon consists in calling the universe home. Can we humans as seemingly insignificant creatures be truly where the universe is heading? Can the human as phenomenon of and for the universe be the key to the universe's salvation? Teilhard believed so and through his eloquence he led me to believe the same.

I see my experience now as one that a prophet, if not a mystic, might experience. It was a vision, I now think, of what is at stake when science is divorced from the spiritual and theology is divorced from the cosmic. *The Garden of God*, paradoxically, grew out of this mystical experience of hell. It is my answer to the question that a view of hell on earth raised within me. As such, *The Garden of God* is an intensely personal book for it actually tries to describe a conversion experience.

My experience of hell on earth brought me to my knees before the Lord of the whirlwind. I learned to become innocent again both before the facts of nature and the dogmas of theology. What is missing in the contemporary Christian tale of salvation is the human place in the cosmos. I can never see theology again without this cosmic lens. Only a cosmic theology of heaven and earth can truly answer the questions raised by a human hell.

Thus, I see *The Garden of God* as a prophet might. It is not only a theological proposal but also a call to repent. We must fall in love with the earth if there is to be a heaven. The key to such a romance are the most beautiful, endless forms that define what we mean by *cosmos*. In such beauty is found the true intersection of heaven and earth. Here the two "hands" of God—Christ and the Spirit—are shaping a new cosmos. It is also in that intersection where the key to the human phenomenon is to be found. That key, I believe, is a place, a place of beauty—indeed, a garden.

These passionate words can get lost in a book too tightly concerned with scholarly details. It is my intention to move the heart so as to guide the mind. For this reason, I have tried to keep the scholarly work as much as possible in the background. More important, this "manifesto" for a theological cosmology crosses many academic disciplines. Much has been said about the proper way to write across disciplines. I plan to use a method I call aesthetic insight that uses a technique called "interlacing." Interlacing is based on a suggestion by Charles Peirce that an alternative way to build an argument is by "reasoning [that] should not form a chain which is no stronger than its weakest link, but a cable whose fibers may be ever so slender, provided they are sufficiently numerous and intimately connected."[1]

"Interlacing" is the artful weaving of various perspectives across disciplines to gain an insight greater than any of its components. It reveals at the same time the fragility of our vision while offering us a greater vision than before. Moreover, "interlacing" deftly weaves across perspectives but is not a perspective *per se.* The end goal of "interlacing" is aesthetic insight, not a new perspective.[2] By aesthetic insight I mean something similar to what Josiah Royce, the great nineteenth-century philosopher, meant by religious insight.[3] An insight, according to Royce, is marked by breadth of perspective, coherence of vision, and personal touch.

An aesthetic insight has all these qualities. It achieves them, however, through what Christopher Alexander, the well-known architect, calls "centers" (about which I will have a lot more to say in the last chapter). A "center" is that nexus of relationships which makes a whole out of many parts. It is not the whole itself. Neither is it the parts. It is that which accounts for an experience of beauty by allowing the parts to be seen as a whole. Aesthetic insight through the technique of "interlacing" discovers the "center" in which many perspectives find a unity that moves the heart. It grasps unity within complexity, but it does so through an experience of beauty. I will be using "interlacing" and aesthetic insight as a method throughout the book as I seek to find the "centers" that make a theological cosmology.

Such a method leads to a certain style of writing that not everyone finds to be their cup of tea. They find the style beautiful but imprecise, saying too much and saying too little, compelling yet irresponsible. To critics of my method and style, I beg forgiveness for giving offense. Yet I believe whole-heartedly that we must begin to see the interconnectedness of the world, to grasp its complexity, even if our intellectual traditions have conditioned us to seek a different type of grasping.

"Interlacing" and aesthetic insight, for all their weaknesses, have this as strength. They seek the insight of interconnections, not the strength of demonstration. If our question is whether we are at home in the cosmos, then I do not know any other method more oriented toward helping us find an answer. For the answer to this question requires grasping a staggering complexity of relationships. It is the nature of that grasping that is the most radical proposal in *The Garden of God*. I begin with the beautiful rather than the true or the good. Beauty, I have found, grasps complexity in a way no other starting point can match.

How the beautiful is grasped, however, is elusive and the subject of the field of aesthetics. Nonetheless, while the nature of beauty may elude us, its experience is accessible to all. Beauty, furthermore, brings a kind of knowledge known only by being enjoyed. This is the nature of the grasp of that which is complex. As such, a book that has such grasp as its goal is a deviation from the academic style of demonstration and argument. Thus, I beg the reader's patience. I am after grasping the immense web of fragile human interconnectedness with one another and with the rest of the cosmos. I believe "interlacing" disciplined perspectives toward gaining aesthetic insight can help us grasp this complex interconnectedness by discovering the "centers" that bring about a place of Beauty on Earth. It is a method, I believe, proper to a garden.

Aesthetic insight is needed if we are to discover the garden of God in the cosmos. As I hope to make clear, gardens are not manufactured but cultivated, their craft a collaboration between ourselves and the earth. They are not so much designed but discovered. The key to cultivating the garden of God is the discovery of those "centers" which issue forth beauty as abundant life. In the course of the book, several centers will emerge from the method of aesthetic insight interlacing elements from the natural sciences, scholastic and contemporary philosophy, art theory, aesthetics, and the theology of Teilhard de Chardin.

These centers include place, heaven and earth, beautiful form, cosmic sacramentals, dynamic formal causality, the "whereness" and "what-ness" of place, the twin human helix of human frailty and abundant life, the fully cosmic Christ and the equally cosmic Holy Spirit. All these will be discovered and developed in what is to follow.

Discovering anew the importance and location of the intersection of life-giving relationships is crucial if Christianity is to meet the challenge of the twenty-first century. That challenge comes to us not as a problematic future but as the re-discovery of our home in the cosmos. To seek that home in the future is misguided. It is already here. Nonetheless, it must be discovered and cultivated.

As such, a theological cosmology is also a spirituality, a falling in love with the earth. Such a love issues forth abundant life and marvelous creativity. Indeed, creating such a garden will mean engaging the most spiritual of our human activities, that is, our creativity. It is my fervent hope that this call for a theological cosmology will be heard by others who are not theologians. In the end, *The Garden of God* may perhaps be best seen as a prayer. May a new collaboration of theology with other disciplines bring about a new kind of spirituality that will discover the road back to our true home in the cosmos—the garden of God.

Acknowledgments

A work of theology is almost always written in community. Often the names of members of this community are hidden. There are some names, however, that must be acknowledged for their generous and able support. First, I want to thank David Ayotte, S.J., Dr. Emily Lyon, Teresa Perez-Martinez, Sung Lee Ho, John Braverman, S.J., Richard Tambwe, S.J., and Patricia Martin. These doctoral students graciously read drafts of the manuscript and gave essential feedback. It is a joy to be surrounded by such young intellects and a blessing to share in their enthusiasm for theological reflection.

I also want to thank Fr. Arthur Poulin, O.S.B. Cam., for his gracious permission to use his beautiful painting *Girasole* on the cover. Fr. Poulin is a gifted artist. *Girasole* captures the spirit that is behind *The Garden of God*. For this, I owe him my deepest gratitude. I also would like to thank the Camaldolese monks at Incarnation Monastery of Berkeley and at New Camaldoli Hermitage for listening patiently to bits and snatches of the work in progress. Their feedback and response helped tremendously in the spiritual direction that *The Garden of God* took in its final form.

Finally, I want to thank Kathryn, my wife, and Sophia, my daughter, for their patience and support. I especially want to thank Sophia for the playful but very profound questions she kept asking about God, the garden, and ordinary life. She may not have realized it then but her questions became a powerful lens that helped focus the direction of the work. To all of these and the many others I have not mentioned, my deepest thanks. You are the flowers that flourish in the bountiful garden of God.

1

At Home in the Cosmos

Are we at home in the cosmos? There is urgency in the question. Whether by nuclear blast and radiation, the alteration of the earth's climate, or the poisoning, even the eradication, of our food supply, humanity has reached a critical point toward mass extinction. Environmental journalist Gary Strieker reports that "there is virtual unanimity among scientists that we have entered a period of mass extinction not seen since the age of the dinosaurs, an emerging global crisis that could have disastrous effects on our future food supplies, our search for new medicines, and on the water we drink and the air we breathe."[1] Indeed, scientists Bradley Cardinale, Marc Cadotte, and Todd Oakley reported at a 2008 meeting of the National Academy of Sciences that the Earth is in the midst of its sixth mass extinction of plants and animals, with nearly 50 percent of all species disappearing.[2]

Perhaps the greatest sign of the question's urgency is that it seems like a new question. Whether we are at home in the cosmos is an ancient question, one that has been asked ever since humans first began burying their dead with food and supplies for a long journey. In the short three or four hundred years of that era we call modernity, however, the question gradually dis-appeared from our cultural consciousness. Raised again in the twentieth century in the midst of great scientific discoveries of great galactic spaces and a world apparently ruled by chance, the question was deemed irrelevant.[3] The human's place in the cosmos was declared insignificant. This, in turn, led to a sense of lost intimacy with the cosmos. Virginia Stem Owens, the cel-ebrated author of spiritual essays, put it this way:

> Space as a mindless, lifeless void had no place in any of man's cos-mologies before the scientific revolution. Before that, not only did the bushes burn, the serpent speak, and the trees clap their hands, but the ether, that vast, ineffable ocean in which we were all sub-merged, trembled with intelligence. Then came the drought, the four hundred years' temptation in the desert. We became accus-tomed to living in a wasteland where life receded steadily from being, and being receded from space. In our collective mind's eye, subject shrank from object. Our feet faltered, the music stopped, we fell out of the tree, the dance was over. The image of Bacon's individual bodies, reduced to external relationships, ruled our imagination.[4]

Owens makes clear how far our sense of loss of intimacy with the cosmos has progressed. Whether we are at home in the cosmos, however, is a question that asks more than our empiri-cal significance in the universe. It is a question of ultimate sig-nificance for the human creature and, even, the cosmos. For asking the question suggests the search for an understanding of the value of human life, the tragic sense of that life, and the promise and hope of a transformed universe, a new creation. This bold claim comes not from the empirical sciences but from Christian belief. As such, it is also a question of ultimate sig-nificance for Christian theology. That the question had for a time disappeared simply points to the sad truth that Christian theology has long lost its bearings under the onslaught of modern and post-modern teachings. We seem to have forgotten that the roots of Christian doctrine reach deep into the soil of cosmic awareness.

Indeed, our present cosmic awareness has taken a paradoxical turn under modernity's influence. A remarkable growth in understanding the forces of nature has led to human culture growing alienated from its natural matrix. A fount of knowledge about the natural world wildly successful in its practical application toward human aspirations and goals ironically has led to an urban culture that destroys its own habitat. In other words, nature and city have come to be at odds with one another. What sort of knowledge is it that enriches our understanding but leads us to self-destruction?

It is the sort of knowledge that enriches our understanding of the cosmos but not of the place of the human in the cosmos. Both the scientific knowledge and the cultural practices that flow from such explorations have shed little understanding on the question of how humans are meant to relate to the natural world. This is unsurprising, for such a question does not lend itself to scientific method or cultural analysis. Asking what is humanity's place in the cosmos is ultimately a theological question, one whose answer depends deeply (but not entirely) upon an accurate understanding of the natural world. Indeed, our very ability to see the natural world around us as a beautiful cosmos requires a bird's-eye view we simply do not possess. We cannot stand outside the cosmos and look at it from the outside to see that it truly is a cosmos. So our sense of the cosmos must come from inside, from deep within our human psyche. It is a deeply personal, profoundly interior sense that transcends our physical locality in time and space to look over at this world we live in and see it as cosmos, a home for us.

Moreover, as Christian belief claims, we are at the same time at home in the cosmos and deeply alienated from it. We were made for the cosmos but then found ourselves at odds with it. We are refugees from Eden. Indeed, we would not be asking the question of being at home in the cosmos if there were not a tragic sense to our existence. We sense ourselves as expatriates and refugees, even in our own home, a tragedy compounded by our simultaneous sense of love for the world around us. The beauty of the universe convinces us it is our home, yet we know ourselves to be far away from home.

To be at home in the cosmos leads us ultimately to ask, What is the meaning of redemption? If, as Paul says, we await a new creation, then our being at home in the cosmos is also a question of the transformation of the cosmos. And this is a question the natural and human sciences are poorly equipped to explore.

Yet theology, equipped as it is to explore it, has apparently avoided the question of the transformation of the cosmos. For instance, in recent years, theologians have concentrated on recovering Jesus' teaching that the reign of God is already here even if not entirely just yet. But it has applied its understanding of that reign almost exclusively to human systems of politics and culture and not to the very land of God's dominion, the creation. And even when it has dealt with the new creation, contemporary Christian theology too often shifts it to the future instead of the present, either by claiming that the future is somehow in the present or simply avoiding the present altogether.

Yet there are signs that theology is beginning to rise to the occasion. More theological voices are raising the need for a theological treatment of cosmology. More studies are being published that show the cosmological roots of Christian doctrine. A vibrant and healthy dialogue between science and theology has been well underway for many decades.[5] This work is part of that chorus of voices now rising to meet the challenge. Are we at home in the cosmos? It is an urgently critical question only theology is well equipped to answer but which will require theology to go back to its cosmic roots and provide us a theological cosmology.

What Is a Theological Cosmology?

First, a theological cosmology is not natural theology, nor is it a theology of nature. A theological cosmology resembles another ancient theological project, namely, Augustine's *City of God*. As in the time of Augustine, Christianity is being blamed for a crisis of tremendous proportions.[6] In Augustine's time, it was the sack of Rome; in ours, it is the sack of the earth.[7] To counter the attacks, Augustine undertook a project to explain God's providential work in history that someday would culminate in a city greater than Rome, the *city of God*. While the analogy between the sack of Rome and the sack of the earth may not be perfect, a theological cosmology promises to be a project very much like Augustine's *City of God*.

Though faced with mass extinction, with the eyes of faith one can see with clarity that we are heading toward a new creation that in some way we are asked to cocreate.[8] Perhaps at this point the analogy breaks down for it is not so much a city we are asked to help build. In fact, it is the metaphor of the city that precisely is being challenged. The city that once mediated between our cultural and our natural existence is dissolving before our very eyes. We are now being placed face to face with the fragile facts of our natural existence. The city can no longer be the human habitat that isolates us from our origins in the dust of the earth. Indeed, the city must either be transformed or it will dissolve. What we will have left may be nothing but a dead, arid desert of cultural monuments to human pride and self-deception.

Let me suggest, then, that it is not a city but a garden that is the context of our redemption. Where Augustine saw redemption culminating in the city of God, I see our redemption culminating in the garden of God. This garden is not so much a future as it is a place. It is not a question of When will we get there? but Where are we going? Putting it this way exposes what has been a classic modern obsession with time that has dominated contemporary theology far too long. As such, it has obscured our traditional connections to the cosmic nature of redemption and imposed a kind of enchantment with modern assumptions passed off as correctives to an older tradition. To see redemption as a matter of place rather than time may help us see with renewed and restored eyes the crucial role that cosmology plays in theology. Where are we going? A theological cosmology ultimately seeks to give an answer. We are going to the *garden of God*, our home in the cosmos.

The Rising Call for a Theological Cosmology

In 1996, theologian Elizabeth Johnson chastised the theological community for its "neglect of the 'cosmos.'" Such neglect, she told us, has compromised the intellectual integrity of theology by failing to look at "the whole of reality in the light of faith." Even worse, such neglect has compromised the moral integrity of theology by blocking what could be a powerful contribution in addressing the "unprecedented ecological crisis" of our "threatened earth."[9] As thrilled as I was then to hear her acknowledge the central role the cosmos has in theology, I do not believe her call has been heeded.

While many theological reflections have been written since Johnson's remarks that address the cosmos, most have dealt either with ecological concerns or with the relationship of science and theology. None of these, however, has had the power to illumine faith and capture the imagination in such ways as can be found in, for instance, the cosmological writings of the great Jesuit scientist and theologian Teilhard de Chardin (whom I will discuss at length below).

Perhaps the reason lies in Johnson's own understanding of the theological project of a turn to the cosmos. She tells us that "Whatever our subdisciplines, we need to develop theology with a tangible and comprehensive ecological dimension. I am not suggesting that we just think through a new theology of creation but that cosmology be a framework within which all theological topics be rethought and a substantive partner in theological interpretation."[10] What is exciting in Johnson's proposal is that she calls for a cosmology that will be a framework for all subsequent theological topics. What is not clear is whether such a cosmology is to be built upon insights from the natural sciences or upon ecological concerns or, even, out of the theological tradition itself. It seems to me that a theological cosmology must include the first two possibilities but must grow out of the last possibility, the theological tradition. In any case, Johnson has done theology a great service. She has pointed out the crucial need for a theological cosmology. Nonetheless, she leaves us with an important question. How is such a cosmology to be conceived?

Elizabeth Johnson is not only who has called for a more comprehensive cosmology. The noted scientist and cosmologist, George Ellis, tells us that while "cosmology is the science that studies the physical structure of the universe," such an understanding of cosmology is much too narrow. He believes that "cosmology refers to an overall world-view that throws light not only on the structure and mechanisms of the Universe, but also on its meaning."[11]

In his book *Before the Beginning*, Ellis outlines what elements such a cosmology ought to include. He lists five "big questions" that have "concerned humanity since the dawn of consciousness." These include (1) the nature of the physical universe; (2) the question of creation, that is, origins; (3) the issue of the final state, that is, ends; (4) the place of humanity in the universe; and (5) the meaning of existence.[12] One can detect in these five questions, however, the three main objects of metaphysics: the universe, the nature of the human, and ultimate meaning or God. It seems Ellis wishes to bring metaphysical questions into the study of the physical structure of the universe. If this is so, then Ellis ought to be commended for recognizing that cosmology asks ultimate questions both of the universe and of the human.

Yet Ellis's project leaves us with questions as well. Does Ellis mean to add metaphysical synthesis to scientific analysis or is he saying that scientific analysis is capable of metaphysical synthesis? If it is the former, Ellis is charting a path similar to Teilhard. I suspect, however, that Ellis means the latter, in which case I fear his project is doomed. The five questions he is interested in asking call for a method of synthesis. To expect scientific analysis, the method of breaking things up into parts in order to understand them, to encompass synthesis, the method of accurately describing the whole of experience, seems overly confident of science's capabilities, if not actually naïve.

While appreciating Ellis's insight into a broader cosmology, I see a theological cosmology being built out of all the possibilities implicit in Johnson's proposal. A theological cosmology can be discerned out of the theological tradition. The tradition, however, is to be informed (but not constrained) by insights from the natural sciences. It should also be oriented toward ecological concerns in such a way that profound insights into humanity's relationship to the environment emerge out of the tradition itself. This calls for a new method that is able to keep in sight all these possibilities and integrate them into a new insight. This is the method mentioned in the preface that I have called aesthetic insight and uses the technique called interlacing. I believe aesthetic insight can give rise to a new cosmological consciousness in theology. Such a consciousness has profound implications.

A true cosmological consciousness in theology would lead us to revisit our understanding of creation so that we may get beyond the doctrine of *creatio ex nihilo*. It ought to revisit our understanding of providence and bring light into our hopes of an abundant life shed of misery and suffering. In other words, it ought to give a robust account of the connection between creation and redemption. This means revisiting the doctrine of the fall and the nature of evil, not just in human affairs but in the universe.

A theological cosmology also ought to give an account not only of the original creation but also of the new. Moreover, it should do so by reexamining what we mean by our belief in the resurrection of the body, wherein the body is not just used as a metaphor. Finally, a revised doctrine of creation must help us understand the way to that new creation, not only as a journey into the future but also as a journey to a place. Our modern obsession with time ought to be corrected with a more biblical concern with place. Our redemption is tied not so much to a time but to a place. Until we make that shift in redemptive orientation, cosmological consciousness in theology will languish.

A theological cosmology, moreover, ought to involve more than borrowing insights from the natural sciences and applying them to theological issues. I do not believe Ellis's view of cosmology as a matter of adding metaphysical synthesis to scientific analysis is viable. Nonetheless, a theological cosmology ought to provide insights into the very nature of the universe itself. This was, after all, the very conviction of those patristic and medieval theologians to whom Johnson so eloquently refers in her appeal for a turn to the cosmos.[13] Most important, however, a theological cosmology must address the question of being at home in the cosmos. This means, I believe, taking another look at our original home in the cosmos so that we may look with fresh eyes at the promised new home. In other words, we must address the nature and role of the garden.

Outline for a Theological Cosmology

So what does this *garden* look like? What are the elements of a theological cosmology? The question of the nature of the universe certainly belongs to cosmology. In theological cosmology, however, the question does not take shape as merely asking about the physical structure of the universe. Theology recognizes that there is something beyond physical structure in the universe. For this reason, theologians have, for the most part, preferred to speak of a *cosmos* rather than a *universe*. This preference refers to the recognition that the whole that is the universe is not a merely physical whole. The "uni" in universe would not, in a theological cosmology, refer to a physical unity. The unity of the cosmos is different. What is the difference? It is beauty.[14]

Cosmos or Universe?
A cosmos is a beautifully ordered unity.[15] As such, a beautiful unity is quite different from a mere physical unity. Bonaventure used the image of a stained-glass window, whose beauty manifests itself when light from the sun shines through it. Though the window is beautiful in itself, its beauty would not be manifest to us without the sun shining through. Such is the beauty of the cosmos. God's glory shining through the window of the universe reveals its beauty, reveals it as cosmos.

If we carry the analogy of the stained-glass window further, one could describe the cosmos also as a window into sacred place, a place that engenders praise and worship. The sense that the cosmos calls for praise of its creator is part of a revised doctrine of creation. The noted biblical scholar Claus Wester-mann, for example, tells us that "Praise of God, the Creator, does not presuppose the creation story, but quite the reverse: praise of God is the source and presupposition of the creation story."[16]

As such, the unity of creation is shown to have a marvel-ous dynamism. It unites our hearts to God. Moreover, it has the double aspect of a liturgical dynamism. The cosmos receives glory and returns praise.[17] Herein is the difference between the two unities. The unity that belongs to the cosmos is more than the unity of a whole. It is a unity made beautiful through its dynamism, which unites the cosmos and ourselves to the very One who made us. The dynamism so eloquently expressed in the big bang theory of the universe does not yet capture the fuller dynamism revealed in the Christian doctrine of creation. The big bang theory can make us gasp at the tremendous power at work in the universe, but it cannot help us see the true source of that power, a marvelous love.

Beyond ex Nihilo, the Ordaining Power of God

A cosmology, says Ellis, ought to give a theory of creation. I am not sure whether Ellis means that a cosmology ought to have a theory of origins or something about a creator. A theological cosmology, for example, has a theory of creation in the doctrine of creation *ex nihilo*, creation out of nothing. It is not, however, a theory of origins. It is a doctrine about the power of God. Indeed, a theological cosmology would point out that in order to understand the source of the power revealed in the physical cosmology that is the big bang theory of the universe, one must consider the nature of divine power.

Theologians in the Middle Ages made a useful distinction in the nature of God's power: they recognized the difference between God's *absolute* power and God's *ordaining* power.[18] God's absolute power answered a particularly vexing ques-tion about the cosmos: Why something and not nothing? It is the power that is behind the *ex nihilo* doctrine of creation. It emphasizes the absolute dependence of all created things on God's will. It is a powerful doctrine that makes clear that the universe, as a whole, is not self-made. It answers the question scientists hesitate to address in the big bang theory: What happened at what scientists call $t = 0$, that is, at the very instant the big bang went off?

Yet such a doctrine of God's absolute power leaves another important cosmic question unanswered: Why is the world ordered this way and not some other way? This question also belongs to a doctrine of creation. It refers to another aspect of God's power, the power to ordain or, rather, to shape the world. This power can be understood in both a static and a dynamic sense. The Middle Ages saw it very much in a static sense. The shape of the world is a done deal. God created a cosmic order that would last until the end time. Perhaps one of the greatest contributions of the natural sciences to theology has been the discovery that the world is very dynamic indeed. But what sort of cosmic dynamism has science discovered?

The Heart of Cosmic Dynamism: Cosmic Love

Perhaps the great astrophysicist Stephen Hawking can help us ask this question more eloquently. At the end of his book *A Brief History of Time* he muses: "What is it that breathes fire into the equations and makes a universe for them to describe?"[19] I have given a hint of an answer above. It is a great love that orders as it unites. Such a love, however, cannot be understood without the tragic note that gives it context. As Paul Santmire put it, there is "travail to nature."[20] There is a struggle in nature herself that includes pain and extinction, suffering and agony. Such travail has been expressed in many religious myths. It is the struggle of order versus chaos. In Christian understanding, such a struggle cannot be described in terms of opposite warring principles. What God created is good. Precisely because it was created good, struggle in nature must be seen in a special light. It is not the struggle of the strong against the weak but the struggle of a new universe being built. This new universe is meant not to replace, but to fulfill and complete, the original. It is the struggle inherent in reconciliation, that is, of a universe becoming reconciled to the loving order of God's cosmic plan. It is the universe struggling to become a cosmos.

There are signs of this struggle everywhere. Scientists, for example, are only beginning to expose the role that chaos and order play in nature. Order is nature's response to chaos and chaos is the creative source of order. Even more significant, this order out of chaos is strikingly beautiful. It is as if at every moment the universe chooses to order itself rather than become a chaotic mass of undifferentiated, static bits of inert matter. This apparent choice manifests itself in a great dynamism of endlessly beautiful forms that come and go with the centuries. It expresses a dynamism akin to spirit. It is the dynamism of a powerful love where chaos and order find reconciliation by forming ensouled bits of matter manifest as dynamic forms of striking beauty.[21]

As such, a theological cosmology goes beyond the *ex nihilo* doctrine. This doctrine has been used to express the absolute contingency of the universe. But another kind of contingency is part of the doctrine of creation. Contingency is also to be found in the reconciling power of God's ordaining love made manifest in the dynamic fragility and beauty of the universe's forms.

The contingency associated with divine power, however, has another dimension not captured in the *ex nihilo* doctrine. Such power created the Garden of Eden. God did not create a generic garden but a particular, contingent, that is, dynamically beautiful garden. In other words, God's creative power wrought not simply beings into existence but a particular place of striking beauty. Creation is not simply about existence but also about a place of existence.

Getting Back to Place

Elie Wiesel spoke of the twentieth century as "the age of the expatriate, the refugee, the stateless—and the wanderer."[22] For one such as me, a Cuban refugee, Wiesel exposes a painful wound. The experience of being placeless is particularly painful and frightening. Wiesel's remarks reveal the pathos inherent in the question: Are we at home in the cosmos? It exposes as well the implicit cosmic pathos one finds in the letter to the Hebrews, a letter written with the exodus in mind.[23] The universe is also a refugee with us. As such, it points out that a theological cosmology is, in part, a theology of suffering and not simply a theology of nature. A theological cosmology must address suffering in a cosmic way. It must help us understand what Paul meant in Romans 8 when he tells us that creation groans to be fulfilled. Suffering, in other words, is the context in which a discussion of the universe's final state must take place.

This context, according to the theological tradition, begins with an expulsion from Eden, a mandated displacement that, throughout the centuries of tradition, finds expression in a longing for a heavenly Jerusalem. Thus, it seems odd that the question of place has disappeared from our inquiries about the nature of our redemption in the cosmos. To be at home in the cosmos is ultimately a question of the meaning of redemption. Yet twentieth-century theology found it easier to speak of eschatology, the end times, than of cosmology, our final place. Such theology posited that the end of our suffering will occur not when we reach a place, our home, but when we end up at a point in time, the future. The future, however, has clouded contemporary theology's understanding of redemption. It needs to get back to place.

In a theological cosmology, place means more than a location or a geography. Place has an interior dimension as well as an exterior dimension. I live at 232 Cherrywood Avenue but it is home to me—it is both exterior and interior in my understanding. In a theological cosmology place takes on a very profound meaning. If the cosmos is seen to include an interior dimension, then place in cosmology includes what the tradition refers to as heaven and earth.

Heaven, in a theological cosmology, does not refer to some spiritual place outside of the creation but is part of the creation itself. It is the invisible referred to in the Nicene Creed.[24] It is the interior dimension of cosmos as place. A theological cosmology gives an account of the relation of heaven and earth and their role in our redemption. This relation is, essentially, the reconciliation of heaven and earth. In this, time is involved, but only as it relates to place. In this perspective, the future is inadequate to explain or even to point to the cosmic interlacing of heaven and earth into the home that is to be our salvation. The time of heaven and earth, of the invisible becoming visible, is not simply the future but also the present and the past. All of time must be invoked to understand the interpenetration of heaven and earth.

The Question of Evil

But heaven and earth as components of a theological cosmology raise questions regarding the interaction between heaven and earth. This was the place where premodern theology dealt with angels and demons. If we can get past the caricatures our modern age has made of angels and demons, we can perhaps recognize the importance of revisiting certain doctrines concerning angels in a theological cosmology.

One of these is the doctrine of the fall of the angels. Found in Daniel and in Revelation, the fall of the angels has been used in theology to qualify and deepen the meaning of the other fall, the fall of the human. The fall of the angels brings evil into the creation right at its beginning. Somehow the mystery of evil is tied in with the very mystery of creation. If Christian belief in the fall of the angels ought to tell us anything, it is that it is insufficient to place evil entirely upon human shoulders. While humans introduced death into the world through their sin, they did not invent evil. Evil was offered to humans by the serpent, and humans accepted it.

The fall of the angels, as Louis Bouyer writes, helps us see the human "by virtue of his creation and its conditions, a first potential redeemer of the world. If he had been faithful to the call of God, who intended him to fill the place left by the prevaricator, his faithfulness would have erased the initial transgression. This is the meaning of paradise, the restoration of the world around man."[25] This view has solid basis in the patristic literature yet has been neglected in contemporary thought, either due to a lack of belief in demons or angels or aversion to the doctrine itself. Nevertheless, the doctrine still has something to teach Christians in the twenty-first century. Evil has cosmic dimensions. We misunderstand its nature if we see it simply as a result of human moral failing. There is something profoundly spiritual in human evil acts that neither law nor reason can curb. The malignant spiritual dimension of evil is ultimately to be found in the human alienation from the cosmos.

Perhaps this lack of awareness about the cosmic dimension of evil explains why theological treatment of human evil and suffering borders on the irresponsible. Much of the contemporary discussion has focused on a dichotomy between "good guys" and "bad guys." In this construction, there is not so much evil as there are bad guys that oppress and harm us. Good guys struggle against these bad guys and eventually overcome them. This dubious characterization of the nature of evil seems naïve and reductive. By contrast, studies concerning trauma victims provide us with a more expansive window into the nature of evil. Why trauma studies? First, they permit us to look at the contemporary Job, innocent people devastated by an evil that is hard to name. Second, they provide a serious look at the nature of evil from an empirical, clinical perspective. As such, it is a fresh view somewhat free of metaphysical assumptions and very helpful in grasping the nature of evil as it appears to us today.

Trauma as a word has its roots in Greek and means "wound." Trauma refers to more than physical wounds. Trauma also refers to wounds that are relational, emotional, psychological, and spiritual. A common way to define trauma is as a state of being overwhelmed physically and psychologically.[26] Understood this way, trauma can be seen as part of normal life. After all, life confronts us regularly by overwhelming us. Being born, for example, is our first traumatic experience. Trauma, then, can be seen as an ordinary element in human experience. If we were to leave the discussion on trauma at this point, however, it would be dangerous. While it is true that in life one is bound to get hurt, it is also true that once hurt one can expect care for one's wounds. A key ingredient basic to life's traumatic experiences is the response of others to an individual's trauma; the nature of their response will determine if such trauma will be healing or destructive. As such, it isn't trauma *per se* that is undesirable but how it is handled.[27] Therapists see in their practices trauma that has not been handled, trauma to which there has been no adequate response. In such cases, victims face lingering trauma, trauma that seems to feed on itself, as we see in those suffering from post-traumatic stress disorder. Such trauma is intrinsically psychological and spiritual.

These studies of trauma victims suggest ways to characterize evil that is more concrete than the metaphysical description of evil as *privatio boni*, the privation of the good. These studies tell us that the attempt to define evil is an attempt to register something solitary and unknowable. In other words, whenever evil occurs, systemic ambiguity, denial, and obscurity attend it.

Evil, as Sue Grand so insightfully put it, "tends to be brazen in its presence and yet radical in its concealment."[28] In other words, evil is "illusory and mysterious and at the same time blatantly obvious and concrete."[29] This means that one must distinguish between trauma and evil. As Means and Nelson put it, "trauma is an event, evil is a process."[30] It is evil, not the trauma, that is destroying the person!

Means and Nelson offer us the following definition of evil:

> Evil creates and builds upon brokenness in the world by threatening, attacking, destroying, and desecrating the integrity of the relational nature of life. Furthering and exploiting the naturally occurring divisions within and between persons, evil leads to increased fragmentation, alienation, and polarization as it turns people against themselves, others, their natural environments, and their God. Evil works against reconciliation and healing and is the chief obstacle and threat to the wholeness and interconnectedness of God's creation.[31]

Evil, then, operates in multiple levels at once: individuals, friends, families, social institutions, cultures, even the natural world itself. Evil destroys more than individuals. This picture of evil is not very different from the image Ignatius gives us in one of the spiritual exercises. Imagine a rock dropping into a pond. The ripples extend throughout the pond. In the same way, a traumatic event ripples through all society, including the natural world itself. If no response is given to this event, the trauma gives rise to a self-feeding process of disintegration and broken relationships.

This understanding of evil, then, helps us understand how important the doctrine of the fall of the angels is to our understanding of the fall of the human. For if we apply the understanding of evil we have learned from trauma studies, then perhaps we might see that the fall of the angels and the fall of humans both revolve around the human place in the cosmos. Original sin is original challenge to find our home in the cosmos, a home made elusive to humanity through the temptations of malignant evil addressing human failing. This challenge is made present to every human generation. The challenge to finding our home in the cosmos subsequently means not simply the restoration of Eden but finding out what makes us truly human. It means loosening the grips of evil on this world by growing ever more human. The restoration of Eden, then, is not a mere return to Eden but a growing ability to respond to the brazenness of evil in the world and to reveal its insidious concealment. The key to our home in the cosmos, of course, is Christ, who came to show us what it means to be fully human and on the cross revealed evil so that it may never fully hide again. But Christ is the word become flesh. And in this doctrine, too, a theological cosmology is necessary to understand its full implications.

The Resurrection of the Flesh

To ask if we are at home in the cosmos is also to ask if we are at home in the flesh. It is flesh that ties the human to the cosmos. Flesh underscores the human as phenomenon. The human as phenomenon emphasizes our foundation in the processes and materiality of the cosmos. We are dirt, we are Adam, but we are dirt given form through the power of God's breath. In other words, we make God's spirit a visible phenomenon through the wondrous dynamic materiality that marks us as human. This is the human phenomenon. Matter matters to God. Matter makes spirit possible. Matter makes spirit visible. Nowhere is this clearer than in the creature called human. Indeed, the human reveals the spiritual orientation of matter in a way no other natural phenomenon can.

On the other hand, it is also flesh that makes it difficult to live in the cosmos. Flesh brings us pain, disease, hunger, thirst, and tears. The frailty of flesh questions our very ties to the cosmos. Indeed, it is flesh that alerts us to a tragic sense to our life in the cosmos. For flesh offers us a paradoxical experience. There is no doubt that we experience flesh as mortal. Yet in that experience of mortality also lies an experience of immortality.[32] That is, we know ourselves not only as mortal but also as immortal. Death is not the final answer for us, nor is it natural for the human creature.

It is this double experience, moreover, that poses flesh as the greatest challenge to Christian faith. Gnostics and a score of ancient and modern heresies challenge Christian faith by attempting to dismiss the paradox. Claims continually are made that either immortality of the human makes flesh an illusion or the mortality of the flesh makes immortality of the human improbable. This paradox cannot be easily dismissed. The sense that there is some sort of existence after death has been held since the first humans began to appear on the earth.[33] For Christians, the challenge can be put in form of a question: What do Christians mean by the resurrection of the flesh?

It is not an easy question for the theologian. It turns on how one understands flesh. Scripture is not very helpful here. The Hebrew Bible speaks of *bāśār*. The great scholar Hans Walter Wolff translated the term as "Man in his infirmity."[34] It refers to the person as a whole but also to what we would call "flesh." Yet if *bāśār* stands for flesh in its physical and material dimensions, it also stands for flesh in the sense of what binds people together, such as the connectedness of a family. Finally, *bāśār* also means the human who in him- or herself is weak and frail, even ethically frail.[35] For this reason, *bāśār* needs God's help. Thus, in the Hebrew Bible, flesh has a variety of meanings around a single consensus: flesh is frail.

The New Testament does not clarify matters. Jesus heals deformities of the body but always associates it with the faith of the one healed. In other words, it is not clear what was the real object of healing, the body or the spirit. Paul continues and even compounds this ambivalence. Capitalizing on the fact that the Greek language has two different words for body, *sarx* and *sōma*, he makes a distinction between the two. *Sōma,* like *bāśār,* denotes the person as a whole and also the physical and material elements that make up a human being. *Sarx,* on the other hand, refers to human frailty and mortality. In Paul's usage *sōma* is the basis of a life with God, *sarx* is a life that separates us from God. In the resurrection, it is the *sōma,* not the *sarx,* which is risen.[36] Ambivalence becomes confusion when, in ordinary translation, the nuances in the Greek language are lost. *Sōma* and *sarx* are often translated as "body" and "flesh." Yet this is not the whole story.

The New Testament retains the Hebrew Bible's characterization that flesh is frail but adds a new component. The need of flesh for God's help finds answer in the word become flesh. Frailty finds God's favor, not God's condemnation. Our understanding of flesh as frail must find answer in the incarnation, God finding favor with the frail. A theological understanding of flesh must begin with Christ. The ambivalence and confusion between body and flesh find their rest here. For if we trace the meaning of flesh through the Christ, we find more clarity on its meaning in the crucifixion, death, burial, resurrection, ascension, and return of the Christ. The frailty of the flesh is the strength of God. These two are inseparable and define our place in the cosmos.

A Theological Cosmology

So, again, what is a theological cosmology? Let me suggest that a theological cosmology attempts to "see" God in all things. It makes visible the inner meaning of phenomena by allowing them to move the human heart. In other words, a theological cosmology is an aesthetics of creation. Like science, it pays attention to the phenomena of the universe, but it also attempts to "see" the inner meaning of all things. A theological cosmology, however, recognizes that for the human there can be no detached observation. Phenomena proper to a cosmos move the human heart. We do not simply observe; we participate.

This understanding of a theological cosmology reflects Teilhard's profound insight that the human is a phenomenon. It also adds, however, the theological insight that the human is not a mere first among phenomena, we are meant to know and love the phenomena in the world, including the phenomenon that we are. Moreover, the cosmos' fate is tied to our own. What ought to give us pause, however, is that we, among all creatures, are meant to see the world as a cosmos. This is not merely a property of our biology. It defines our place in the cosmos. We were meant to restore goodness and justice to the world. Now, because of the fall, it is our own goodness and justice that are also at stake; but the essential mission has not changed. Evil is not to have its way in the world.

Christ came that our mission be finally accomplished. He sent us the Holy Spirit to renew the gift of our humanity that we may heal the trauma ever present in the universe. Together with Christ through the Holy Spirit, we are to restore Eden in the reconciliation of heaven and earth. We are to be reunited with God in Eden because God did not mean to stand outside of God's own creation but to dwell in and inhabit it. God means to live with us in a cosmos that reflects and allows all creatures to participate in God's own goodness and life. Our ability to see a cosmos is our ability to experience God's presence in all things. This is not pantheism. It is not even panentheism. It is the garden of God.

2

The Human Phenomenon

Teilhard de Chardin's New Significance

Former senator Harris Wofford recounts the following story concerning Sargent Shriver's nomination acceptance speech at the 1972 presidential campaign:

> Then in the presidential campaign of 1972, after George McGovern asked him to become his running mate, I was helping Sarge work on his acceptance speech. He was late, as sometimes happens—the motorcade to go to downtown here in Washington to the special convention to nominate him to hear his acceptance speech was revving up. Sarge was still unsatisfied with the end. "I know how I want to end!" he suddenly proclaimed. "It's Teilhard de Chardin. I'm going to find that quote. It's on a plaque in a pile upstairs." We physically tried to stop him, but he bounded out and in two minutes was back with the plaque. So he ended his address with these words of Teilhard that brought the quite electrified delegates to their feet: "The day will come when, after harnessing the winds, the tides, and gravitation, we shall harness for God the energies of love. And on that day, for the second time in this history of the world, man will have discovered fire."[1]

The influence of Teilhard de Chardin is hard to overestimate. As Wofford's story shows, Chardin's thought crops up in the most unexpected places. The eloquence and breathtaking sweep of his thought has touched the hearts of innumerable people. Yet, in spite of his popularity, his works remain controversial within the Roman Catholic Church. Teilhard had been silenced in his lifetime for his writings. In 1962 a *monitum*, or official warning by the Vatican, was given on the posthumous publications of his works. Yet something remarkable happened in the early part of the twenty-first century.

On February 15, 2008, Cardinal Schönborn, Archbishop of Vienna, came to the Graduate Theological Union at Berkeley, California, to give an account of his new book on evolution and theology, *Chance or Purpose?*[2] As a respondent on the panel, I was a bit apprehensive, knowing that the cardinal had caused a bit of an uproar the previous year. He had made some comments regarding evolutionary theory that were reported by the *New York Times*. I was both flabbergasted and moved when he told us of a story he had planned to use but was unable to include in his book. It was a story about a little girl who in 1955 had met an old man in Central Park who made quite an impression on her. She returned the next day to show him one of her prize possessions, a fossilized Ammonite spiral shell. When the old man saw it, his eyes lit up and, tracing his fingers around the shell, he said, "Ah, the spiral of the earth!" The little girl returned the next day but the old man was not there. In fact, she never saw him again. The old man happened to be Teilhard de Chardin. He had died shortly after he had seen the Ammonite fossil the girl had shown him.

The cardinal appeared to be truly moved as he told the story. Could it be, I asked myself, that the church is finally seeing the wisdom in Teilhard's thought? Schönborn's remarkable words regarding Teilhard in *Chance or Purpose?* suggest as much. He calls Teilhard a "witness to Christ" who "dared a venture that was at the same time full of risks yet necessary."[3] After so many years of suspicion, what happened? Has the church begun to reconsider the value of Teilhard's thought? Has the time come for Teilhard de Chardin to become relevant to the official teachings of the Roman Catholic Church? I believe Teilhard holds a new relevance for today, and not just because a high-ranking cardinal views him favorably.

As I argued in the previous chapter, the time for a theological cosmology has come. Teilhard de Chardin gives us an example of a powerful and persuasive theological cosmology emerging out of a collection of insights and argumentation that takes the form of an ellipse with two foci: (1) the human and his or her place in the cosmos and (2) Christ and his significance for both humanity and the cosmos.[4] Any future theological cosmologies will need to begin there but offer their own insights. This means more than revitalizing his thought in the twenty-first century, since there still exist within it serious theological problems and loose ends that need addressing. I hope to advance a new theological cosmology by bringing new considerations to these two foci of Teilhard's thought that will make clear his new relevance but also point to ways in which his thought can be advanced. As a scientist, Teilhard knew that no hypothesis or theory can stand still. If he had lived into the twenty-first century, he surely would have continued refining and advancing his original insights, and would have welcomed this spirit of science applied to his pioneering theology.

Complexity, Interiority, Christology, and the Cosmos

Teilhard was a prolific writer. Although not systematic, he was a profound thinker. I do not intend to give a full exposition of Chardin's thought in this brief introduction. I merely wish to introduce a few major aspects of his thought that are relevant for a theological cosmology. Even this modest goal may be difficult to achieve. The first sentence in Teilhard's *The Phenomenon of Man*, however, goes a long way toward fulfilling that goal: "This work may be summed up as an attempt *to see* and to *make others see* what happens to man, and what conclusions are forced upon us, when he is placed fairly and squarely within the framework of phenomenon and appearance."[5]

What happens, asks Teilhard, if we consider the human creature as a phenomenon of nature? One would think this is a poor way to start a look at the human. Doesn't it mean that the critical element of what makes us human, our self-consciousness, gets lost in the nonintelligent phenomenal structure of nature? Doesn't human spirit along with all things spiritual disappear in scientific accounts of nature? Not with Teilhard. By asking the question of the human as a phenomenon he also is asking, What is really the phenomenal structure of the world?

The human, according to Teilhard, is "the key to the universe."[6] Human spirit, manifest in self-consciousness, marks the human not as a unique phenomenon in nature but as the exemplary phenomenon of nature. This means that the natural world is marked by a decided drive, an evolution, toward greater and greater consciousness. That consciousness reaches a peak in the human phenomenon where it becomes self-consciousness. This bold claim is the heart of Teilhard's scientific vision. More than any scientist in his day he saw that to understand matter, one would have to begin to understand spirit.

Spirit for Teilhard is a drive toward closer union, which is the process of life itself, with life being a matter of seeing or consciousness. As he puts it, "the history of the living world can be summarized as the elaboration of ever more perfect eyes within a cosmos in which there is always something more to be seen. . . . To try to see more and better is not a matter of whim or self-indulgence. To see or perish is the very condition laid upon everything that makes up the universe."[7] Thus, Teilhard the scientist begins with the spiritual to understand the very fabric of the universe. But how does spirit become manifest as natural phenomena? Teilhard answers, closer union, the essence of spirit, means two things when applied to natural phenomena: *complexity* and *interiority*. Nature is marked by a double drive toward greater complexity and deeper interiority.

Living creatures, for example, are marked by a striking complexity. Teilhard observes that ever-growing complex structures marked the evolution of living creatures. On the weight of this observation, Teilhard proposes that evolution of creatures followed a law toward greater complexity. Such complexity is the result of a drive to closer union at work in the universe. But greater union has one other consequence. It means greater consciousness or interiority. Thus, along with the law of greater complexity, Teilhard adds the law of greater interiority. By starting with the human as the exemplary phenomenon of nature, Teilhard proposes the laws of greater complexity and interiority as the principles of a grand evolution on a cosmic scale.

These laws are Teilhard's greatest scientific contributions. Unfortunately, few scientists of his day saw it that way. Teilhard's starting point, the human, is not where science would have started. Science's exemplary phenomenon of nature is not the human but matter. The human, then, would have to be some sort of phenomenon of matter. It is no wonder, then, that Teilhard was severely criticized in his day for his evolutionary theories. It also explains why his scientific thought was almost lost in the waning days of the last century.

Teilhard's starting point of the human for his science naturally suggested a starting point for his theology. I am referring, of course, to Christ. If the key to the universe is the human, then the key to the human is Christ. Teilhard, however, was hampered by the Christology he had inherited, which was worked out in the Middle Ages in the context of a static view of creation.

Who would Christ be, asks Teilhard, if the world were not static but coming dynamically to life and consciousness through an evolutionary process?

Teilhard sees in Paul's letter to the Colossians an answer: "And he holds all things together" (Col. 1:17). Christ thus becomes for Teilhard the unifying force of the entire cosmos. This means that Christ is also the energizing principle that gives the universe its drive to closer union. But where is the cosmos headed? To whose union is the universe coming ever closer? Teilhard answers: it is Christ, the omega point of evolution's aim and goal. Thus, Christ, for Teilhard, becomes the unifying, energizing, and completing principle of the entire cosmos. In Teilhard, it is not so much that the universe is human centered but it is Christic.

Teilhard's Christology, too, fell under much mistrust in his day. A Christic universe makes holding on to a historical view of the fall problematic. A Christic evolving universe also calls into question the nature of sin and evil. Is our suffering simply part of a learning curve toward greater self-consciousness? Is evil merely apparent since whatever evil people do the drive to union with Christ is still a sure thing? Christ as omega point also raises questions about the nature of the end times. How does Christ "come back" to judge the living and the dead if he is already there waiting for us at the end times? Finally, where is the Holy Spirit in Teilhard's Christology? Has Teilhard so christified the universe that there is no place for the Holy Spirit in the evolutionary process?

Teilhard's Christology raises these and many other questions. Whether they are insuperable, time will tell. The questions that Teilhard's Christology raises are crucial if the church is to continue into the twenty-first century with a viable view of Christ. More important, Teilhard's insights can help, in part, answer these very important questions. As such, Teilhard's Christology may be more valuable to the church for the questions it raises than the answers it provides. For in having raised the truly crucial questions of the church's faith in a twenty-first-century world, Teilhard has proved himself to be a true doctor of the church.

As noted above, Teilhard's theological cosmology has two main foci. One of these is considering the human as a phenomenon of nature. Essentially, this means asking the question of the relationship between the human and the cosmos. The other focus is the relationship of Christ to the cosmos. The question to ask now is, Has anything changed that would make us see these two elements in Teilhard in a new light? Can one bring new considerations to each of these parts in the twenty-first century? The answer is most definitely yes! Indeed, perhaps nothing has changed as much as our understanding of the cosmos since Teilhard's time. Likewise, the questions that Teilhard's Christology raises can no longer be ignored. The time has come to take a new look at Teilhard.

The Relationship of the Human and the Cosmos

Let's take a look at the first element of his theology, the relation of the human to the cosmos. This relationship can be seen to consist of three parts: the cosmos, the human, and the relationship between them. It is important then to explore each of these parts individually.

The Cosmos
In terms of the first part, the cosmos, much has changed in our understanding. As mentioned above, perhaps the most famous insight of Teilhard's cosmology is his hypothesis that the matter in the universe evolves toward higher complexity and interiority.[8] There is, he says, both a "without" and a "within" to matter, an exterior and an interior aspect that increased in intensity

through evolution. This hypothesis, especially the one concerning the interiority of matter, was considered "unscientific" in Teilhard's day.

It has become increasingly evident to biologists that the question of complexity in living organisms cannot be ignored by science. The problem can be seen clearly in this comment by molecular biologists J. Cohen and S. H. Rice:

> Molecular biology has set itself the task of looking for the fundamental pieces with which the biological jigsaw is to be put together. Not surprisingly (but with surprising efficacy), it has found many of them, and there are certainly more to come. Once found, these pieces can be arranged on a page next to one another in a reasonable sequence, and . . . Behold! An organism! Well, not quite.[9]

This "not quite" reveals the weakness of the reigning scientific epistemology which holds that knowing the "parts" is sufficient explanation of the "whole." It is becoming increasingly clear that this epistemological paradigm is in deep trouble when it comes to understanding biological systems.

Another scientist, Stuart Kauffman, asks in his book *At Home in the Universe,*

> Whence cometh all this bubbling activity and complexity? Ultimately, it must be a natural expression of a universe that is not in equilibrium, where instead of the featureless homogeneity of a vessel of gas molecules, there are differences, potentials, that drive the formation of complexity.[10]

This consideration prompts Kauffman to note that no theory in physics, chemistry, or biology has yet explained complexity. Thus, he feels "we must think anew."[11] This means getting beyond the reductionism of present science. This reductionism stems from two presuppositions. The first, derived from Galileo and succeeding physicists, is the view that reality ultimately consists of particles moving in a void. The second presupposition holds that "explanations for higher-order entities are to be found in lower-order entities."[12] But these presuppositions are beginning to fail science.

If all explanations go downward from the highly complex to the least complex, then it seems logical that once you have reached an explanation by explaining the least complex, one can then go upward from there and explain the next, higher complex. Yet that is not the case. Kauffman asks,

> But if all explanatory arrows point downward, it is something of a quiet scandal that physicists have largely given up trying to reason "upward" from the ultimate physical laws to larger-scale events in the universe. Those downward pointing explanatory arrows should yield a crop of upward-pointing deductive arrows. Where are they?[13]

The bottom line in these debates is that science is coming to grips with the phenomenon of the complex whole in nature. In doing so its basic presuppositions are being shaken to the core. This means that science is beginning to recognize that complexity is a basic phenomenon in the universe and perhaps its most profound. This means that science is about to have a paradigm shift. Kauffman aptly puts it: "We truly need a new worldview [beyond reductionism]. We must rethink evolution."[14]

The presuppositions of the science of Teilhard's day are rapidly coming to an end. In its new struggle to understand life, science has begun to accept what Teilhard had proposed over half a century ago: complexity is a basic feature of the universe. If nothing else, this development in science ought to encourage us to take a new look at Teilhard. It appears that his science was ahead of his time. Could it be possible that the significance of Teilhard's thought has yet to be properly evaluated?

Let's take a look, then, at the other law Teilhard proposed for the cosmos. Does interiority exist not merely in the human but in all of nature? I had the privilege to work on a joint project with Mark Graves, a systems scientist associated with the University of California at Berkeley, and Carl Neuman, who at the time was the team leader of the developmental biology department of the European Molecular Biology Laboratory at Heidelberg, Germany. What I saw at Neuman's laboratory took away any doubt from my mind about the universality of interiority in the world of nature.

Dr. Neuman showed us a remarkable set of experiments that had been designed by one of his colleagues, Darren Gilmour, concerning the development of the dorsal stripe of the zebrafish embryo. Dr. Gilmour is known worldwide for his mastery of time-lapse photography at the cellular level. He played us a video clip showing a line of cells (the dorsal stripe) being formed by a group of "leader" cells creeping along the side of the developing zebrafish embryo. Dr. Gilmour then had a laser beam cut and separate the "leader" cells from the line of cells they had been guiding. He expected the "leader" cells to keep moving, blindly unaware of their separation. He was, however, shocked to see that the separated "leader" cells stopped as if they had become aware of the separation, then began moving back toward the separated line of cells. The "leader" cells extended a single cellular strand and touched the separated line. The "leader" cells then began moving in the same direction as before. The line of cells began to follow, eventually closing the gap and becoming one single line again![15]

This experiment cannot be easily explained in terms of blind, efficient causes. There was a clear sign of "awareness" by these cells and a clear sign of communicating that awareness. Given that these cells do not have brains, Teilhard's contention that the universe possesses different degrees of interiority and mindfulness then gains new credence. If some scientists shunned Teilhard in his day, it was because Teilhard's insights into natural reality were ahead of his time. Today, scientific field after scientific field is showing the wisdom and insightfulness of his thought.

The Human

If cells exhibit mindlike behavior, then what about the phenomenon called human? To those in the humanities it may seem trivial to assert that humans have a mind, yet if one asks the question with the human seen as a natural phenomenon, the answer becomes more elusive. Indeed, here is the source of the nature and culture divide that has driven us to an unprecedented natural crisis. For if human self-consciousness cannot be verified as phenomenon, then there truly is a chasm between culture and nature, city and garden. But if human self-consciousness can be verified as a phenomenon, the gap between culture and nature threatens to vanish and human self-consciousness melts into the trillions of natural processes as one more insignificant activity of a vast universe.

Teilhard sees these as unacceptable choices concerning the human phenomenon. He asserts that human self-reflection is more than a seamless, continuous development, yet less than an unbridgeable gap in evolution. Teilhard argues that evolution reached a new level with the arrival of the human creature, an anthropogenesis of conscious self-reflection. For the first time in its ancient history, the universe could reflect back on itself.[16] As Teilhard so eloquently puts it, "After a million years of reflection, there is a dynamic meeting in the consciousness of man between heaven and earth at last endowed with motion, and from it there emerges not simply a world that manages to survive but a world that kindles into fire."[17] Thus, human self-consciousness is unique and special in the universe. It comes from the processes of the universe itself, yet it is no mere phenomenon, one among many. Human self-consciousness is the aim of evolution and the key to understanding the universe. Needless to say, Teilhard's view has met stiff resistance. But is the situation changing?

Interestingly, considerable research has taken place among the neurosciences and in psychology into the phenomenon of human self-consciousness. David Hay, a zoologist, explores the thesis in his book *Something There* that "spirituality is part of the mainstream of our human experience, rooted substantially in our physical nature, what we are as biological organisms."[18] This spiritual awareness emerged out of the evolutionary process and is creative in that "it operates through acts of conscious choice . . . [and] in the sense that . . . the human species have a hand in their own evolution."[19]

But how do you explore this thesis empirically? Spirituality is notorious in being difficult to define. Yet if it is to be seen as phenomenon a definition that makes available empirical investigation is necessary. David Hay attempts to solve the problem by noting that although "pinning spirituality down to an agreed definition is impossible, [all participants in the study] were able to recognize it when they came face to face with it."[20] Using this pragmatic definition Hay and his collaborators were able to identify such moments in practice. This gave Hay a way of defining spirituality as "Awareness of the Here-and-Now, Awareness of Mystery, and Awareness of Value."[21]

"Awareness of the Here-and-Now" is an explicit form of spirituality practiced by Buddhist monks and Christians having to do with what the French Jesuit Jean-Pierre de Cassaude called the "sacrament of the present moment." "Awareness of the Here-and-Now" finds empirical significance in a most startling fact. It is the awareness universally found in infants. Indeed, the other two types of awareness, of mystery and of value, are found empirically in the curiosity and wonder of children. By studying the different awareness present in infants and children, Hay and Rebecca Nye , Hay's associate, have come to identify a core category that fits the data they had gathered on the spiritual awareness of infants and children. It is *relational consciousness.*

This came as a surprise to these two researchers for their picture of spiritual life "was someone sitting in a lotus position in hermit-like isolation."[22] The relational nature of spirituality became confirmed for Hay when subsequent studies surfaced "what mothers have always known. . . ; that you can have a conversation with an infant."[23] Emese Nagy in the 1990s showed dramatically that meaningful interaction happens between mothers and infants shortly after birth.[24] These studies demonstrate that "the physical and emotional intimacy of relationship both inside and outside the womb is intense and it is immediate. It is very obvious that the biological process of becoming a human being is the extreme opposite of an isolated, abstract affair. It is here, in this most natural of processes, that relationship and relational consciousness is made manifest as the primordial mode of being-in-the-world."[25]

In other words, human spirituality, that unique and very special mode of "being-in-the-world" that defines us, is rooted in the very cosmic process of our birth. Hay's work, along with other psychologists on spirituality, does come with a caveat. Hay's empiricism tends to blur the distinction between spirituality and consciousness. One striking difference that might distinguish the two is the sense that spirituality is not simply an awareness but an actual union with something or someone greater than our awareness. But it may be that Hay's understanding of consciousness is reductionistic. That is, consciousness may well be something much greater than mere awareness.

In either case, Hay's findings support Teilhard's bold claim as to the special role the human plays in the cosmos and gives it new credence through these empirical studies. Ridiculed by many in his time, perhaps Teilhard was ahead of his time. More important, he has become suddenly relevant again to any theology that wishes to address the question of being at home in the cosmos.

The Relationship Itself

We now come to the third element of Teilhard's first focus in his elliptical theology, the relationship of the human to the cosmos. Perhaps Teilhard's most controversial claim, at least to scientists, is also the starting point of all his theology: that the human is key to the cosmos. The picture of the universe revealed in the twentieth century is one of vast, unimaginable distances filled with innumerable stars and galaxies. Given this view, how could anyone suggest that a fragile creature in a small planet not even the size of a star could be of much significance in the universe? Yet scientists are coming to terms that the fundamental constants which make this universe the vast void filled with stars too many to count has an undeniable human reference. It is known as the cosmic anthropic principle.

Most scientists have long taken it as axiomatic that the Copernican cosmological revolution also knocked off the human from a self-appointed chair at the center of the universe. This axiom is now beginning to be questioned. Brandon Carter, an Australian physicist known for his work on black holes, suggested at a cosmology symposium in 1974 that "our location in the universe is necessarily privileged to the extent of being compatible with our existence as observers."[26] While this proposal may seem trivial, it has tremendous implications in our physical understanding of the universe, for it implies that the intelligibility of the universe reached at through human observation can only be understood if it is seen as being founded in nothing less than the universe observing itself![27] What is striking about this proposal is its similarity to a metaphysical statement, though it is not strictly an *a priori* statement, such as found in metaphysics. It has an empirical basis.

One of the most important discoveries of twentieth-century physics is that the "sizes of stars and planets, and even people, are neither random nor the result of any Darwinian selection process from a myriad of possibilities."[28] The gross size and structure of all the constituents in the universe are due to a set of cosmic constants that limit the possible numbers of equilibrium states between all and any of the forces operating in the universe. Yet because of these constants life evolved in the universe and a phenomenon called human becomes aware of the constants themselves. What modern physics has yet to do is explain why these numerical cosmic constants have the values that they do. For if they vary by even the most infinitesimal amount, there would be no stars, no planets, no life, and no human observer to record the tragedy.

Leonard Susskind, a physicist at Stanford University and discoverer of string theory, explains it well:

> Man's place in the universe is also being reexamined and challenged. A megaverse that diverse is unlikely to be able to support intelligent life in any but a tiny fraction of its expanse. Many of the questions that we are used to asking such as "Why is a certain constant of nature one number instead of another?" will have very different answers than what physicists had hoped for. No unique value will be picked out by mathematical consistency, because the landscape permits an enormous variety of possible values. Instead the answer will be "Somewhere in the megaverse the constant is this number, and somewhere else it is that. And we live in one tiny pocket where the value of the constant is consistent with our kind of life. That's it! There is no other answer to that question." The kind of answer *that this or that is true because if it were not true there would be nobody to ask the question* is called the anthropic principle. Most physicists hate the anthropic principle. It is said to represent surrender, a giving up of the noble quest for answers. But because of unprecedented new developments in physics, astronomy and cosmology these same physicists are being forced to reevaluate their prejudices about anthropic reasoning.[29]

The cosmic anthropic principle has become a real scientific insight guiding scientific research into the nature of the universe. It also brings new relevance to Teilhard's most important work, *The Phenomenon of Man*.

It appears that Teilhard, the scientist, was ahead of his time. His claims about the nature of the cosmos, the nature of the human, and the relationship of the human to the cosmos find surprising resonance in contemporary scientific research. This new relevance heralds, I believe, not simply a new life of theological reflection based on Teilhard's thought but also a paradigm shift in science itself as it comes closer and closer to the spiritual dimension of the universe, a dimension Teilhard had long foreseen. Now, however, it is time to look at Teilhard the theologian. By this I mean taking a look at the possible relevance of the second focus of his elliptical theology, the Christ. Is there new relevance for the Christ at the heart of matter, the cosmic Christ of point omega?

The Christ

On October 13, 2006, the Congregation for the Doctrine of the Faith (CDF)[30] issued a notification warning against misleading theological conclusions by Father Jon Sobrino in his book *Jesus Christ, Liberator*. I was asked to give a response by the magazine *America*. While the notification pointed to various errors the CDF perceived in Sobrino's book, the methodological question caught my eye. As I wrote in *America*,

> The methodological storm centers on the nature of the "setting" that determines a starting point and overall reference for a Christology. Sobrino emphasizes the social setting defined by the "Church of the poor"; the Notification identifies it as the "faith of the Church." The clash centers on the very nature of the relationship of Christ

and the Church or, in other words: Can Christ be loosed from the Church?[31]

The CDF apparently is warning that Sobrino's Christ is being wrenched from his ecclesial matrix. What is feared is that a Christ that emerges out of a social setting instead of a communion of faith is a Christ subject to political and ideological currents that have little interest in faith. Indeed, Sobrino's method of taking the social context as the ecclesial matrix out of which the Christ emerges may lead to an unabashed theological pluralism.

A Christology in Crisis

Let me suggest that the notification on Jon Sobrino manifests the symptoms of a Christology in crisis. It is not so much Sobrino that caused the crisis but that he has correctly identified it. The church of the twenty-first century must think anew its ecclesial identity. Is the Christ of the church also the Christ of the world? If so, then does not an ecclesial self-understanding that sees the Christ as its personal possession place Christ under institutional house arrest? On the other hand, is the Christ of the world also the Christ of the church? Can Christ be yanked out of the matrix of apostolic faith to take on as many faces as there are people, the result being his not having a face at all? I believe this twin dilemma can only be solved by a responsible doctrine of the cosmic Christ.

The Roman Catholic Church of Vatican II, in my opinion, is showing signs of its age. Vatican II helped the church come to terms with modernity. Modernity, however, has long passed. The church now faces a world that is rapidly becoming globalized and human fortunes intertwined in an unprecedented way. The believer can no longer detach oneself from the unbeliever, the rich from the poor, the theist from the atheist, the Hindu from the Christian, the New Age practitioner from the

Benedictine monk. All our lives, lives of belief, unbelief, and different belief are irrevocably intertwined and we must live a life of communion that transcends the particularities of our respective faiths.

What Christ shall guide us in this brave new world? What Lord shall help the disciple navigate a life of faith outside the ecclesial milieu? These questions cannot be answered by a Christ who only makes sense within an institutional setting. They can neither be answered by a Christ that has no institutional grounding. They can only be answered by the cosmic Christ, the one whom winds and seas obey and the one to whom every knee shall bend in heaven and on earth. This is the cosmic Christ. It is the Christ, I believe, of the twenty-first century.

A Christ for the Twenty-first Century

But is Teilhard's Christ the cosmic Christ of the twenty-first century? The answer is not a simple one. Teilhard's Christ is a cosmic Christ, but one that is easily assimilated and manipulated from recognition as the church's Christ. I do not believe this means that Teilhard's cosmic Christ is fundamentally flawed. I do believe it means that Teilhard's Christ suffers from the lack of a language and categories to describe him that a new cosmology demands. Teilhard did not leave us a failed Christ. On the contrary, it means Teilhard left the church a legacy in christological thinking that may someday flower as a new era in theology.

So who is this cosmic Christ and what has to be done to make him the church's Christ? Right off, one must say that Teilhard did not invent the cosmic Christ but inherited him. The cosmic implications of the risen and now ascended Christ became significant to many of the writers of the New Testament. The Pauline letters, the Gospel of John, and Revelation explicitly recognize this cosmic dimension of the Christ. The cosmic Christ later developed in the writings of many of the church fathers such as Clement,

Origen, Maximus the Confessor, and many others. Beginning in the late Middle Ages and reaching a nadir in modernity the tradition on the Cosmic Christ all but disappeared.[32] It was Teilhard that recovered the tradition in the twentieth century. His major achievement and his genius was reinterpreting the tradition in the context of the new view of a dynamic, interconnected, relational universe the natural sciences had discovered.

Given the great silence of several centuries on the cosmic Christ tradition, it is a wonder Teilhard was able to speak of it at all. What ought to strike us as more than coincidence is the role the natural sciences played in revitalizing this ancient but vital tradition. If it had not been for the marvelous view of the universe the natural sciences discovered, the church might have lost a tradition crucial to her faith. Indeed, the dynamism, complexity, and interconnectedness of this newly discovered universe helped us discover an aspect of the significance of Christ that goes beyond expiation for our sins. Teilhard was the first of his generation to see this. The task, however, proved daunting. What language do you use to describe the cosmic Christ when the only language you have inherited only describes a static and unrelated cosmos?

The methodological question now becomes clear: either one must invent new terminology or bring new life to traditional terminology that has been forgotten. Teilhard depended largely on the former option but perhaps the time has come to consider the latter option. Teilhard's use of the language of spheres, genesis, energy, centers, and omega point certainly fit the view of the universe discovered by the natural sciences. I do not believe, however, that Teilhard was effective in constructing a bridge to the older language of the cosmic Christ. If he had, I believe his cosmic Christ now seen in light of a new cosmos would easily have been recognized as the church's Christ. The question now becomes whether it is possible to build that bridge starting where Teilhard left off.

Where Is Jesus Now?

Let me suggest that the way to build that bridge is to ask a pertinent cosmological question concerning the Christ of the church: "Where is Jesus now?" As such, it becomes not only a christological question but one that addresses the cosmic implications already within christological doctrines. It also has relevance to our understanding of the church for wherever Jesus is, so is the church. This means that doctrines of the church also have a cosmic dimension. Finally, answering the question above will take us into language at once traditional but also new. In other words, it reveals the power of traditional language to speak anew in the twenty-first century. So, let us begin: Where is Jesus now?

The Relevance of the Ascension
Teilhard's Christology could be said to be the persistent raising of the question: Where is Jesus now? As such, it is surprising the short shrift he gives to the doctrine of the ascension. That doctrine has much to do with the traditional terms of heaven and earth, which come to us through the Cappadocians and the Nicene Creed, tying the creation with the ascension. God, Creator of heaven and earth, Maker of the visible and the invisible, now has the risen Christ in glorified body ascended and sitting at his right hand. It is the doctrine of the ascension that strongly implies the cosmic Christ. Heaven is not a reality outside of the creation. The ascended Christ did not leave the universe but is now at the helm of the forces that shape and direct the universe. It is a divided universe, however. The forces that shape and direct the universe are the forces of reconciliation and interpenetration of heaven and earth.

This is not to say that Teilhard did not have an ascension theology. For him, ascension was not simply a movement upward but also forward. With Christ-the-Evolver at the helm, evolution is taking us upward and forward to the omega point where a new form of life awaits us. Seen this way, it is plausible that Teilhard could have employed the traditional language of heaven and earth. In not doing so, Teilhard missed an opportunity to develop his theology more fully. For example, Teilhard lacks a theology of the Holy Spirit in his evolutionary framework. Yet one of the key elements in the doctrine of the ascension is the coming of the Holy Spirit to make present on earth the ascended Christ in heaven. It is here where Teilhard could have profited greatly with a fuller theology. For it is here where the roots of *ecclesia* grow.[33]

If we ask the church the cosmological question—Where is Jesus now?—the answer has both an earthly and a heavenly dimension. Jesus has ascended to heaven. He, however, is now made present to the church on earth through its Eucharist and the action of the Holy Spirit. In other words, the cosmic Christ is to be found in heaven. His presence on earth, however, is mediated through the Holy Spirit. Thus, in a divided universe, where heaven and earth are not yet one, the cosmic Christ is present in the cosmos both as a eschatological (heaven) and pneumatological (earth) presence.

It is the church's Eucharist that reveals this double cosmic presence. *Sacrosanctum Concilium*, for example, tells us, "In the earthly liturgy we take part in a foretaste of that heavenly liturgy which is celebrated in the holy city of Jerusalem toward which we journey as pilgrims, where Christ is sitting at the right hand of God, a minister of the holies and of the true tabernacle."[34] This theology of the Eucharist where heaven and earth come together both in an eschatological sense but also in the here and now of the liturgical action has its foundation in the doctrine of the ascension.

It seems to me that Teilhard's moving and profound *Mass of the Earth* was missing this double cosmic sense, the *epiclesis* of the Holy Spirit. Yet it is precisely here where the cosmic

Christ is to be seen as the church's Christ. Nonetheless, *Mass of the Earth* is not totally flawed. It reveals something about the *ecclesia* forgotten in modernity, that the church like its risen, ascended Lord has a cosmic dimension. It is one, holy, catholic, apostolic, and cosmic. If Teilhard failed to make clear the role of the Holy Spirit in the cosmic Christ, the church in modernity failed to recognize its cosmic nature.

A Matter of Place Not Time

The second element toward building that bridge between heaven and earth is the traditional theme of the land. Walter Brueggemann, in his groundbreaking book *The Land*, argues that "an inordinate stress on *covenant* to the neglect of *land* is a peculiarly Christian temptation and yields to a space/time antithesis."[35] In other words, Christian emphasis on salvation history as opposed to inheriting the land does not jibe with either the Old Testament or New Testament witness. Salvation is more than emancipation. As Brueggemann puts it, "separation from community but location within it, not isolation from others but placement deliberately between the generation of promise and fulfillment."[36] This restoration of the physical meaning of what the Synoptics call the kingdom (or dominion) of God, John calls eternal life, and Paul calls inheritance should alert us to the crucial significance of the cosmic Christ.

The dominion of God cannot be delocalized. It is not space. It is not even a time such as the future. It is place. What is place? Here, Brueggemann is worth quoting in full:

> "Space" means an arena of freedom, without coercion or accountability, free of pressures and void of authority. . . . But "place" is a very different matter. Place is space which has historical meanings, where some things have happened which are now remembered and which provide continuity and identity across generations. Place is space in which important words have been spoken which

have established identity, defined vocation, and envisioned destiny. Place is space in which vows have been exchanged, promises have been made, and demands have been issued. Place is indeed a protest against the unpromising pursuit of space. It is a declaration that our humanness cannot be found in escape, detachment, absence of commitment, and undefined freedom.[37]

It is not hard to see, then, how Israel's journey through the desert to the promised land in communion with God becomes, in the New Testament, the human journey through the cosmos to a new creation enabled by the Holy Spirit who makes the risen, ascended Christ present and who now sits at the right hand of the Father. Let me suggest that in the New Testament the themes of land, rootedness, and exile become the theme of finding a home in the cosmos.

Seen this way, perhaps aspects of Teilhard's system such as his soteriology may not be so objectionable. Noel Roberts, for example, accuses Teilhard of assimilating Christ-the-Redeemer to Christ-the-Evolver, that is, "he gave primary emphasis to the creative aspect of Christ's role than to the redemptive aspect."[38] But if the theme of journeying to the promised land is understood as the theme of the cosmos evolving into a new creation, then the creative element is crucial to the redemptive. The antithesis between creation and redemption is ill founded. Perhaps Teilhard's fault lies in emphasizing the future without a corresponding emphasis on place.

A Place of Beauty

The third element in building that bridge is beauty. The language of beauty in traditional theology is one with the language of creation. The church fathers loved to quote Wisdom 11:20 ("But you have arranged all things by measure and number and weight") in their theology of beauty. Indeed, beauty has played a significant role in theologies of creation up to modern times.

Then beauty seemed to disappear from theological reflection. As Hans Urs von Balthasar put it,

> No longer loved or fostered by religion, beauty is lifted from its face as a mask, and its absence exposes features on that face which threaten to become incomprehensible to man. We no longer dare to believe in beauty and we make of it a mere appearance in order the more easily to dispose of it. . . . We can be sure that whoever sneers at her name as if she were the ornament of a bourgeois past—whether he admits it or not—can no longer pray *and soon will no longer be able to love.* . . . In a world without beauty . . . the good also loses its attractiveness. . . . Man stands before the good and asks himself why *it* must be done and not rather its alternative, evil. For this, too, is a possibility, and even the more exciting one: Why not investigate Satan's depths? In a world that no longer has any confidence in itself to affirm the beautiful, the proofs of the truth have lost their cogency. In other words, syllogisms may still dutifully clatter away like rotary presses or computers which infallibly spew out an exact number of answers by the minute. But the logic of these answers is itself a mechanism which no longer captivates anyone.[39]

A universe without beauty cannot be called a cosmology. Nor can a doctrine of creation without a reference to beauty captivate our attention. This means that beauty must also play a crucial role in a doctrine of the cosmic Christ.

Theological Aesthetics

The answer to the question "Where is Jesus now?" has led us to consider certain gaps in Teilhard's theology. The role of the Spirit and of place is certainly notable in Teilhard's system by its absence. On the other hand, I believe Teilhard did have a sense for the role of beauty in his cosmology. But where is it? As usual with Teilhard, the answer is not so simple. There is this marvelous reflection in *The Heart of Matter* concerning the beauty of creation:

> It was thus that the light and the colours of all the beauties we know shone, with an inexpressible iridescence, over the face of Jesus, itself unmoved. I cannot say whether it was an expression of my own wishes or whether it was the choice of Him who determined and knew my tastes; but one thing I know, that these countless modifications, instinct with majesty, sweetness, and irresistible appeal, followed one another in succession, were transformed, melted into one another in a harmony that was utterly satisfying to me. And all that time, beneath this surface movement—both supporting it and concentrating it in a higher unity—floated the incommunicable Beauty of Christ.[40]

Teilhard's stunning description of the beauty of the natural world coupled to the beauty of Christ is an example of what might be called a theological aesthetics.

Theological aesthetics is a relatively recent development in theological reflection. The term itself was coined by Hans Urs von Balthasar, who gave it magisterial content in a multivolume work, *The Glory of the Lord*.[41] Following von Balthasar, theologians began to use the term to define a way of doing theology that takes the human response to beauty as its starting point.[42] Perhaps the most concise and best definition of theological aesthetics comes from theologian Richard Viladesau. Theological aesthetics considers "God, religion, and theology in relation to sensible knowledge (sensation, imagination, and feeling), the beautiful, and the arts."[43] Though brief, the definition indicates how powerful theological aesthetics can be as an approach to problems that defy articulation via ordinary language. As Pseudo-Dionysius noted in *The Divine Names*, the closer we come to naming the reality of God, the less adequate ordinary language becomes.[44] Thus, extraordinary language, the visual, music, the arts are a more adequate way to name the reality of God. Theological aesthetics recognizes this aspect of theological reflection and attempts to understand how these forms of sensibilities to beauty offer us a kind of sensible knowledge about God.

For these reasons, I believe if one could detect a theological aesthetics at work in Teilhard's reflections, a dependence on sensible knowledge that informs his thought, then perhaps one can make Teilhard speak again in a new voice, the voice that emerges from the beautiful. So is there a theological aesthetics in Teilhard? Few commentators on Teilhard have explored this question. There is a striking passage, however, in *Hymn of the Universe*, that can be nothing else but an aesthetics, in which Teilhard, speaking of a friend who has tragically died and been buried at Verdun, describes a stunning vision of "Christ in the world of Matter."[45]

Teilhard's aesthetic-mystical vision of Christ reveals a little-commented-upon aspect of his thought: its aesthetic underpinnings. Teilhard's describes Christ's beauty radiating like light through the world of matter. In doing so it both dissolves its multiplicity and at the same time highlights them. As such, it is strikingly similar to Bonaventure's aesthetics as found in his major work, *Journey of the Mind to God*.[46] For Bonaventure, light is the most spiritual of all creatures. As such, light mediates between matter and spirit, bridging oppositions between bodies. Indeed, light comes from heaven, penetrating the shapeless earth and expressing itself as inward unity and beautiful color in a variety of forms. In other words, light brings unity to multiplicity of forms even while it expresses itself as a multiplicity of forms.[47]

Furthermore, Bonaventure sees light as not only informing the eye, but also forming the eye.[48] In other words, light is not only expressive but also impressive. It not only expresses form but also impresses form. Light, then, enters the human soul, melting it like wax and impressing the form it carries directly onto the soul. The soul impressed by form now feels compelled to express what has been impressed. It seeks an *ek-stasis*, a coming out of itself. But where shall the soul go to express itself in *ek-stasis*? Light, coming from heaven, provides a path for the soul's expression, a journey of ascent to God where it can express its *ek-stasis*.

Here Teilhard differs from Bonaventure. Teilhard's soul, in his vision, descends into the heart of matter, rather than ascending into the heart of heaven. Light, for Teilhard, does not come from above earth but from within earth. But there he finds the heart of Christ. In Teilhard, the light that shines through earthly forms while at the same time creating them is the light of the transfigured Christ. As such, Teilhard's transfigured Christ is also Bonaventure's heavenly Christ, but Teilhard sees heaven not above the earth but within the earth.

As in Bonaventure, light brings forth beautiful forms in Teilhard's aesthetic cosmology. Unlike Bonaventure, however, these forms have a special dynamism. They issue forth in life and consciousness. In other words, the light emanating from Christ's transfigured face does not make its forms merely expressive; rather, it vivifies. The beauty expressed in these beautiful earthly forms is expressed through their life. Indeed, in the experience of beauty illumined by the transfiguring, vivifying light coming from the Sacred Heart of Christ, Teilhard experienced once again the life of his dear friend now buried in Verdun.[49]

It is this fundamental experience that is the heart of an implicit aesthetics in Teilhard's thought. Beauty not only is experienced as life, but gives life. Beauty has the character of light, but it is vivifying light that transfigures matter into beautiful forms. These forms, however, are not static like the ones in Bonaventure. They are living, dynamic forms, their beauty grasped in the movement of their life in the universe. This means that beauty comes, as in Bonaventure, from the light of Christ who is in heaven, except that for Teilhard that light comes not merely from a heaven above to end restfully on earth below, but from heaven at the heart of earth radiating forcefully into the future. It is this vivifying beauty that brings both to Teilhard and his friend "light and peace."

Teilhard, in a sense, gives aesthetics a material dynamism not seen in Bonaventure. The cosmos is not a mirror of Christ's beauty. Rather, it is the life of beauty. Teilhard's aesthetics can be summarized by Gerard Manley Hopkins's phrase in his celebrated poem "Pied Beauty," where beauty "fathers-forth." Christ's vivifying light of beauty fathers-forth an evolving universe that will someday emerge as a new cosmic form of life. The beautiful forms of this earth come from a beauty in heaven found within but also at the end of space and time.

In this aesthetics Teilhard's cosmic Christ can be seen to be as well the church's Christ. For inasmuch as the church also fathers-forth beautiful forms that give life, the cosmic Christ and the church's Christ are one. The beauty to be found in the cosmos is the beauty to be found in the church. By making this connection, I believe a new relevance can be made of Teilhard's cosmic Christ. For if the beauty of the cosmic Christ is found to be the same as the beauty of the church's Christ, then a new cosmic Christology can be built on the foundations of Teilhard's dynamic aesthetics of Christic, vivifying light. In the beautiful, vivifying forms that are to be found in and emerge out of the church, one may find the sacred heart of matter creating an oasis of life in a difficult and deadly world. Indeed, one may find the garden of God.

Summing Up

Any contemporary attempt to propose a theological cosmology must begin with the work of Teilhard de Chardin. Reviled in his day for both his science and theology, Teilhard is resurfacing as a thinker ahead of his time. His views on evolutionary theory are finding empirical support in contemporary science and his revival of the cosmic Christ tradition may be the only way the church will be able to make sense of her identity in an increasingly global and religiously interconnected world.

Nonetheless, Teilhard's theology needs revision. I believe he would have welcomed this not simply as a theologian but also as a scientist. Every scientist knows his work is built on the critical revision of another. This theological work is no different. I do not wish to provide an alternative to Teilhard's work but, rather, a deepening of it. My proposal is that Teilhard's work would profit by asking a pertinent cosmological question: "Where is Jesus now?" The answer to that question brings three new dimensions to his Christology—the notion of place, the relevance of the ascension, and the role of beauty.

The notion of place would shift his science from a preoccupation with the future to a more biblical engagement with land. The relevance of the ascension to the cosmic Christ leads to the second element in my revision of Teilhard's theological cosmology. There is no full doctrine of the cosmic Christ without a corresponding doctrine of the Holy Spirit. While it is the cosmic Christ that may be drawing all things to converge onto him, He does so through the power and dynamism of the Holy Spirit. As the Lord and Giver of Life, the Holy Spirit defines the nature of this convergence: it is the coming together of a place of abundant life. The Spirit also helps us see how the cosmic Christ is the church's Christ. Just as the Holy Spirit defines the cosmic Christ, she also defines the church through the Eucharist. The Eucharist, in other words, becomes a mark of the cosmic Christ in the world. Thus, the church may be said to be not only holy and apostolic but also cosmic.

The Holy Spirit, in turn, leads to my third proposal for a revision of Teilhard's theological cosmology. Beauty is the most visible sign of the work of the Holy Spirit. It is also one of the defining characteristics of a cosmos. Of course, seeing beauty this way means we will have to revise our notions of beauty. This will be explored below. More important, it shows that a theological cosmology has its foundation on a theological aesthetics. Teilhard, I believe, had an implicit aesthetics but it needs to be developed. It is here where I hope to make a significant contribution in the proposed revision.

Teilhard de Chardin may not have gotten everything right in his proposed theological cosmology but he did see one thing clearly. If the church is to regain its prophetic and eschatological voice in our world today, it must develop a convincing cosmology. I am proposing such a cosmology is a place of beauty, built with the help of the Holy Spirit where abundant life is offered by the cosmic Christ who ascended into heaven but is returning by reconciling heaven to earth. It is, in other words, the details of the journey to the garden of God.

3

Heaven and Earth

Is cosmology science or theology? The answer, of course, is both. Yet Teilhard, in his cosmology, took both disciplines to uncomfortable territory. For example, he loosed evolutionary theory from the boundaries science had given it—that is, life on earth—and expanded its territory to include the universe. In doing so, he took evolutionary theory out of the range of scientific orthodoxy—that is, Darwinian natural selection—giving it a direction and a conscious capacity to adapt to natural circumstances.[1] Teilhard did the same for theology. Applying his evolutionary outlook to his faith, he took doctrines of the fall, sin, evil, and redemption to new and sometimes uncomfortable territory as well. While there are plenty of critics on either side of Teilhard's interpretations of evolutionary theory and theology, the point is that a theological cosmology is more than science applied to a theology of creation or a theology of creation applied to science. There is a tension between science and theology inherent in any theological cosmology, a tension that mutually interprets both the theories of science and the doctrines of theology. Any theological cosmology needs to address this tension.

Is Nature or Theology Enough?

What is the nature of this tension? The methodological questions raised by two respected scholars in the science-and-theology dialogue may provide a way to get at an answer to this question. Roman Catholic theologian John Haught, on the one hand, asks the question, Is nature enough?[2] Physicist-theologian Robert Russell, director of the Center for Theology and the Natural Sciences, on the other hand, asks, Is theology enough?[3] These two questions, I believe, reveal the heart of the methodological issues at work in a theological cosmology.

Haught argues that the naturalist presuppositions of science cannot give a full account of the cosmos. Naturalism is expressed in Carl Sagan's famous line: "The Cosmos is all that is or ever was or ever will be."[4] Haught, as theologian, disagrees. The cosmos cannot by itself give an account of itself. For example, scientific cosmology cannot give an account of critical intelligence in the universe. He notes that science can only advance by intelligent beings being open, critical, and intelligent to what is. Yet this cognitive confidence cannot be explained by naturalism. It is an act of intellectual faith. As he puts it, ". . . any coherent grounding of our cognitional confidence—that is, of the trust we spontaneously place in the desire to know and the mind's imperatives . . . can be found only in the mind's native anticipation of a transcending fullness of truth that has already grasped hold of us but which also escapes our grasp."[5] Since Haught believes that mind is continuous at all levels of reality in the universe, such anticipation is not limited to human minds but also to natural process. Here is where theological explanation is necessary. Theology's role is to "make ultimate sense of the anticipatory aspect of nature and mind. It can give a good reason for the existence of a realm of potentiality that allows the world to be anticipatory."[6]

Russell, on the other hand, is more optimistic about the cognitive grounds of scientific cosmology. He recognizes reductionism in science but also in theology. He sees the main inspiration for his work in looking "for a closer relation between theology and science [that does not] continue to restrict science to a secondary role in theology. . . . [Is there] any appropriate way for theology to influence choices made toward scientific research?"[7] Russell's answer to this is his proposal for Creative Mutual Interaction between science and theology. Creative Mutual Interaction (CMI) is a synthesis of methodological suggestions from philosophers of science and religion Ian Barbour, Arthur Peacocke, and Nancey Murphy.

Barbour has demonstrated an analogy between scientific and theological rationality suggesting the fruitfulness and possibility of interaction. Peacocke, in his Gifford lectures, gave a schematic as to how antireductionism could be avoided in science if different epistemic levels are acknowledged in approaching increasingly complex natural realities, each epistemological level being constrained by the level below it. Theology, thought Peacocke, functions at the highest level of complexity. Finally, Murphy suggests theology adopt a research methodology proposed by the philosopher of science Imre Lakatos. Lakatos demonstrated a general philosophical structure to the way actual scientific research is done. He called this structure a research program. Murphy demonstrated the plausibility of adopting such a research program to theology.

Creative Mutual Interaction combines all three into a novel and powerful methodology. Inspired by Murphy and Barbour, Russell turns CMI into an interdisciplinary research program inspired by Lakatos. Thus, CMI is more than adopting a scientific research methodology by theology, or science adopting theological insights, but a research methodology in which science and theology are inextricably combined. Inspired by Peacocke, Russell sees theology at the top of an epistemological hierarchy maximally constrained by scientific discoveries yet able to deal with concepts not reducible to science. Thus, Russell appears to be saying that while theology is maximally positioned to deal with cosmology, it is not enough. It must be constrained by scientific discovery.

What is striking about both positions is the large amount of common ground held between them. Both Haught and Russell adamantly oppose reductionism by science. Both believe that theology cannot be credible if it does not take into account the discoveries of the sciences. Both also believe that theological concepts cannot be reducible to science. In other words, both are saying that a cosmology needs science and theology. They differ, however, in their estimation of which discipline constrains the other. Haught appears to be saying that theology, having the wider view, necessarily constrains the interpretation of scientific discovery. Russell, on the other hand, while allowing that theology has the wider view, would have theology constrained by the discoveries of science.

Haught and Russell differ, however, in their methodological starting point. Russell, intensely interested in the science and religion dialogue, has a strictly epistemological methodology. He begins with questions about knowing reality. Haught, on the other hand, begins with metaphysical considerations. He begins with reasonable beliefs about the nature of overall reality in order to guide his knowing. Here lies the crux of the tension. Which is the horse that pulls the cart? Does one begin with *a priori* beliefs about reality or *a posteriori* knowledge of reality?

The tension is crucial in a cosmology. If cosmology is, in great part, a holistic view of reality, then it has an undeniably metaphysical dimension. A cosmology is not something one can point at and say "there it is." A cosmology is believed. It is *a priori* to our knowing it. On the other hand, reality in the particular, isolated patches of reality that impacts human experience whether by the senses or by instruments, must be discovered.

It is known *a posteriori*, discovered through human experience. Such experience is crucial in discovery. But discovery, as Kuhn in his book *The Structure of Scientific Revolutions* points out, is akin to conversion.[8] It triggers belief. This belief then becomes the filter through which subsequent experience is interpreted.

Thus, belief and discovery, a view of the holistic one and the experience of the particular many, the *a priori* and *a posteriori*, follow upon each other's heels. Belief sets the context for discovery; discovery triggers belief. One needs a cosmology already in place, if one is to discover something new within it. On the other hand, discovery can drastically alter our cosmology believed. Another way to put this is to say that in cosmological thinking, one cannot easily separate epistemological claims from metaphysical beliefs. This interconnectedness of epistemology and metaphysics must be considered in the above proposals by Russell and Haught.

If one follows Russell's method of Mutual Creative Interaction and constrains theology's view of the universe to responsible epistemological claims of science, then the metaphysical assumptions behind those claims go unguarded. Science, however, tends toward a monist metaphysical view of the universe. For theology, a monistic metaphysics is not acceptable. Theology recognizes important metaphysical distinctions between matter and spirit, body and soul. Thus, if theology were to follow Russell's MCI method, then it is not clear what alternative it has but to accept scientific knowledge yet arbitrarily deny the metaphysics such knowledge presumes.

On the other hand, theology unchecked by science's monistic assumptions can find itself dangerously veering toward a dualistic view of the universe. Theology's greatest challenge is how to explain evil in light of an all-powerful and benevolent God. Dualist theological claims crop up in every generation forcing theology to reconsider its metaphysical assumptions in the doctrine of creation.

Scientific knowledge with its monistic assumptions can seem attractive to theologians trying to battle such dualisms. Yet the monistic price of scientific knowledge seems too high for theology to accept without qualification. Haught finds a *via media* to this theological problem. He would have us constrain science with a metaphysical *a priori* that avoids a dualist view of the universe. What is not clear in Haught's approach is whether such a starting point can allow science the radical freedom in epistemology science needs for its method. It is this radical freedom that gives scientific knowledge its respect and authority. To lose it would be to lose all that is worthwhile in scientific knowledge.

Russell and Haught, then, demonstrate the inavoidable tension. Either we constrain theology with the epistemological fruits of science at the price of fighting a monistic metaphysics or we constrain science with metaphysical *a priori* at the price of asking science to give up its radical freedom in epistemology. Let me suggest that this tension has no clear interpretation as long as we do not recognize the problem as a variation of philosophy's One and the Many. The problem can be put this way: How can we connect our particular experiences of reality to the one real universe that exists?

Let me suggest that not all avenues of approach have been tried when it comes to applying the problem to cosmology. So far the epistemological foundation of science, the experience of particular reality, has not taken seriously the experience of Beauty. Beauty has been understood classically as unity-in-variety.[9] As such, it is an approach to the problem of the One and the Many that is congenial to both science and theology. Scientists, on the one hand, often choose between competing theories on the condition of beauty. Beauty also possesses a radical freedom that is one with scientific discovery. It is in its freedom gift-like and revelatory.[10] Theologians, on the other hand, recognize that one of God's names is Beauty. Moreover, theology has a long tradition of reflection on beauty. More important, few scientists and theologians will deny that beauty reigns in our experience of the universe. Let me suggest that starting with beauty rather than epistemology or metaphysics may bring about a new way to discover a viable cosmology.

If beauty is to be our starting point, then one must recognize what is one of its most important characteristics. Beauty is experienced above all as a gift. If one allows that the universe through its beauty is also a gift to be received, then the epistemological and metaphysical divide may be bridged. It is what makes reality a cosmos and not merely a universe. Beauty, let me claim, allows us to see the cosmos not only as a *datum* to be understood but also as a *donum* to be received. In this, it is one with the theological tradition.[11] The donum of the cosmos comes to theology not merely through the doctrine of creation but also through the doctrines of the incarnation and ascension.[12]

The doctrine of the creation, for example, reveals an important aspect of God's relation to the cosmos. Although God transcends the cosmos, God created the cosmos with an immanent rationality that allows the cosmos to be known out of its own natural process.[13] The doctrine of the incarnation, furthermore, tells us that God, who transcends natural process, nonetheless chose to enter natural process to come into an intimate relationship between the cosmos and Godself. In the incarnation, God opens Godself to the cosmos that God may be known intimately and lovingly.[14] Finally, in the doctrine of the ascension, we have the reverse of the incarnation. If in the incarnation God opens up Godself to the cosmos, then in the ascension, Christ opens up the cosmos to God.[15]

Thus, in the creation, God gives the cosmos its own rationality and dignity. In the incarnation, God opens up Godself as gift to the cosmos. Finally, in the ascension, the cosmos is opened up to God. Such is the *donum* character of the cosmos—its dignity and rationality, its capacity for intimacy with God, and its capacity to be transformed by God. The cosmos, then, is a *given* open to inquiry but it is so because it is also a *gift* that gives knowledge, profound intimacy, and abundant life. These three are known as gifts because of their beauty. The *donum* character of the cosmos is immanent in the beauty that is the cosmos.

It is in this *donum/datum* structure of the cosmos where the difference lies between a strictly scientific cosmology and a theological cosmology. Science takes as starting point the cosmos as *datum*. Theology, on the other hand, takes as starting point the cosmos as *donum*. More important, while science has no obligation to incorporate the cosmos as *gift* into its knowledge, theology must come to understand the cosmos as *given*. In other words, theology's doctrines begin with God's gift of grace but they presuppose the given of nature.

At this point it is important to understand that the *donum/datum* nature of the cosmos is not in the form of a dualism. They are, rather, dual aspects of the one cosmos. The *donum/datum* structure prevents the creation from being a mere monistic universe and allows the possibility of a beautiful cosmos stunningly coherent in its breathtaking breadth of living forms. It also avoids God's transcendence of the cosmos from being the dualist opposite of God's immanence in the cosmos. The *given* of the cosmos has become open to God as *gift* and God has become open to the *given* of the cosmos by becoming *gift* to the cosmos.

As such, a theological cosmology is not simply an act of the intellect but also an act of faith. This means that a theological cosmology insists that *both* science and theology take into account the *donum* character of the cosmos.[16] Faith would have no less. Cosmology, above all, is a vision of a gift that redeems. As such, cosmology means more than a unified theory of natural reality or a natural theology. Because both its epistemology and metaphysical foundations are based on the beautiful, theological cosmology is essentially an aesthetic work, for that is the only way a gift can be truly appraised. A theological cosmology, then, is a theological aesthetics of creation.

The Need for Salvation

As we have seen, the doctrines of creation, incarnation, and the ascension are crucial in understanding the *donum/datum* structure of the cosmos. Thus, it may come as a surprise that the present science-and-theology dialogue has concentrated on attempting to answer a single question regarding the character of the cosmos: Where is the universe headed? Thus formulated, it becomes a question of eschatology, that is, the doctrine of the end times, not one of creation, incarnation, or the ascension. As the distinguished physicist John Polkinghorne puts it:

> The ground bass in the discussion [over the eschaton] is the necessity of an interplay between continuity and discontinuity in speaking of God's purposes beyond the end of history. Without that element of continuity, the story of the eschaton would simply be a second story, with no coherent connection with the presently unfolding story of this creation. . . . Without an element of discontinuity, however, that second story would simply be a redundant repetition of the first.[17]

If scientific cosmology is interested in telling the story of the present unfolding universe, theological cosmology would also add the story of a new creation. Scientific cosmology, however, can speak of a discontinuity in the universe only in terms of singularities such as cosmic annihilation or separate parallel universes. Theological cosmology, on the other hand, cannot depend on singularities. It must account for an original creation being transformed into a new creation keeping in tension a "discontinuous continuity" between the two.

Yet to see eschatology as simply the problem of addressing the tension between continuity and discontinuity in the end times ignores the basic issue addressed in eschatology: the need for salvation. This brings a new dimension to be considered in eschatology. While the question of salvation does deal with time, it also deals with place. Indeed, much of the traditional theological discussion on eschatology also includes a spatial dimension. What are the spatial aspects of eschatology? They are what Paul called heaven and earth. Given the crucial role that Paul plays in theological thought on eschatology, it is striking that few of the participants in a recent science-and-theology dialogue on eschatology seriously addressed this spatial divide.[18] One who did was Hans Weder and his reflections are revealing:

> Theological cosmology, then, does not function as a means of over-coming and leaving the world in order to rise to the high spheres of the Creator, but rather it serves to draw attention of human beings to the dignity and inviolability of the things that exist, that all can see. Theological cosmology is concerned with the foreground of the world, not with the background of heaven, and here is the point where theology and natural science meet.[19]

Weder's remarks are remarkably apt when seen in the light of Paul's address to the Colossians. Here Paul addressed Christians who believe that through fasting and ascetical practices they would reach or have a vision of the heaven promised at the end times. One can hear Paul's concern clearly in this passage:

> If with Christ you died to the elemental spirits of the universe, why do you live as if you still belonged to the world? Why do you submit to regulations, "Do not handle, Do not taste, Do not touch"? All these regulations refer to things that perish with use; they are

simply human commands and teachings. These have indeed an appearance of wisdom in promoting self-imposed piety, humility, and severe treatment of the body, but they are of no value in checking self-indulgence. (Col. 2:20-22)

Colossians reveals the prevailing Greek cosmology at the time the letter was written, which consisted in a metaphysical opposition between the realm of eternal being, heaven, and the phenomenal world of death, earth.[20] The Colossians had reworked this cosmology into their Christian eschatology with disastrous results to a proper understanding of Christ's redeeming message. Given the context, one would expect Paul to argue as Hans Weder. Orient yourself to the things of the earth and leave heaven in the background. What is striking is that Paul does not deny the need of a heavenly orientation. In fact, he gives it renewed emphasis!

To understand Paul's response to the Colossians, one has to be aware not of Greek, but Hebrew, cosmology. As Andrew Lincoln, the scholar of Paul's eschatology, describes it:

Paul's view of heaven was derived ultimately from the opening statement of the OT. "In the beginning God created the heavens and the earth" (Gen 1:1). Created reality had two major parts. That part known as the heavens could be thought of in terms of the atmospheric heaven (e.g. Ps 147:8) or firmament (e.g. Gen 1:7,14). As the upper part of the cosmos it also came to stand for the dwelling place of God, pointing beyond its own createdness towards transcendence (e.g. Ps 2:4). Not only so, but the upper limits of the firmament were regarded as concealing a presently invisible created spiritual order (e.g. 2 Kgs 6:17; Job 1:6; Zech 3:1).[21]

Paul added a decisive element to that traditional view: the resurrection and ascension of Christ to heaven.

The Ascension

Christ's ascension has two far-reaching theological implications in Paul. First, heaven becomes more than an abode or an invisible realm. It is caught up in the drama of redemption that involves the Father who sent the Son; the Son who became flesh, was crucified and died, then rose and now ascended; and the Holy Spirit who makes those baptized in Christ present to him and him to them. For this reason, the cosmos as heaven and earth is important and "not to be thought as a static backdrop because it is caught up and involved in the drama [of salvation unfolding in Christ]."[22]

Second, the life of heaven is to be brought to earth. This extends the scope of redemption from the human to the cosmic. It also means that the invisible spiritual is to become intertwined with the visible earthly. Given this view of the cosmos, cosmos as heaven and earth, Paul tells his Colossian friends that because we on earth are united to Christ in heaven we can now live a life of grace. There is no need of earthly regulations or practices that know nothing of heaven.

Here is where Weder's remarks seem discordant with Paul's eschatological reflections. Heaven is the heart of eschatology, for grace is the gift through which the new eschaton shall be realized. In other words, eschatology is more than a way to explain the tension of a continuity and discontinuity in creation. It is also a way to highlight the presence of the already-here and not-yet dominion of God. It is this presence that provides eschatological tension. It is the tension not merely of time but also of place. Thus, the tension of a continuity/discontinuity in time is qualified by a continuity/discontinuity in place. This continuity/discontinuity in place is framed in terms of a cosmos groaning in labor as its heaven interpenetrates and interlaces its earth. The cosmos is a divided land groaning to be reunited again.

A divided land, however, is not a dualistic cosmos. The already-here but not-yet reflects a dynamism of reconciliation, not a conflict of dual principles. In other words, heaven and earth are not dual principles in conflict with one another. Heaven and earth are regions of the one land that have been separated through sin. To those who might still see this as a dualism, I would point out that, in Paul, eschatology reveals the crucial role of grace. Grace allows us to live in Christ risen and ascended to heaven. This Christ is now reconciling heaven and earth taking the cosmos to a redeeming end that, ultimately, is a place, a place where every tear shall be wiped away. For these reasons, the framework of heaven and earth is not to be seen as a dualism. It is no more dualist than the relationship between nature and grace.

Whatever Happened to Place?

Pauline eschatology prevents the end times from becoming merely a matter of time. It is also a matter of place. But what is place? This question has become a central one in the study of human geography, with deep implications for our understanding of what it means to be human. The field of human geography, for example, first began its study of place by concentrating on individual places, or regions, describing their locations and boundaries, and the human practices and meanings associated with those places. As it developed, human geography saw that the particularity of these geographical regions stems from more general underlying social, economic, and political processes. Whatever place is, it is a sort of social product. But why would such immense social, economic, and political energy be spent in producing a particular place? In trying to answer the question, human geography came to the realization that place is not so much socially constructed as it directs social, economic, and political energy toward development of place. Thus, the field came to face its greatest insight and challenge: there appears to be something about place that is primal to human existence.[23]

This discovery truly challenges the field of human geography. That place and human existence have some sort of primordial connection is the stuff of metaphysics, not geography. Yet it is a connection that human geographers cannot evade. Thus, it was inevitable that the primality of place discovered by the field of human geography would be noticed by philosophers. Edward Casey, for example, is a philosopher who has spent a long time exploring this primal connection of place and human existence. He begins his book *Fate of Place* by remarking that

> Whatever is true of space and time, this much is true of place. We are immersed in it and could not do without it. To be at all—to exist in any way—is to be somewhere, and to be somewhere is to be in some kind of place. Place is as requisite as the air we breathe, the ground on which we stand, the bodies we have. We are surrounded by places. We walk over them and through them. We live in places, relate to others in them, die in them. Nothing we do is unplaced. How could it be otherwise? How could we fail to recognize this primal fact?[24]

How could we, indeed?

Casey's observation is not unknown to theology. One of the greatest challenges in early Christian theology was how to speak of the creation, incarnation, and ascension in terms of place. After all, how can one conceive of the creation if not as a place? How could one speak of Jesus born in Bethlehem and raised in Nazareth without a sense of place? How could one speak of Christ ascended into heaven, if heaven is not a place? Yet how can a God who transcends space and time and place be thought of as being *in* a place? To answer these questions the church fathers inherited from Greek philosophy understandings of place that were not entirely suitable as answers to these deep questions. Greek philosophy offered variations of the receptacle or container view of place, that is, "an inert environment in which things happen."[25]

Plato, for example, concerns himself more with space (*chora*) than place (*topos*). He sees space as "simply that in which . . . events occur, a formless and passive medium . . . that does not give shape or determination to what is found in it."[26] Thus, space is not determined by measurement but in terms of the events taking place within it. Since events involve changeable, visible, sensible copies (of archetypes), space must act as the receptacle of these copies while at the same time separating the invisible, eternal, permanent archetypes of ultimate reality. Space, then, allows the copies to become visible and thus rationally apprehended, creating a bridge to the world of the invisible archetypes.[27] What Plato so insightfully points out is that to think of a world separated from or beyond the visible, one must think spatially, for separation is a spatial notion itself.

Aristotle, on the other hand, speaks of space and place almost simultaneously. He sees place as a bounded container into which and out of which things pass.[28] Here we see a different way of handling the transient and the permanent. Aristotle demands a point of absolute rest if one is to understand motion or change. This point of absolute rest becomes the immovable boundary of the container. As such, the container provides a way to measure and thus understand the things that come in and out of it. In other words, place is like a volume that has spatial magnitude. What is important in this receptacle understanding of place is that time becomes irrelevant. Unfortunately, it is this understanding of place that medieval theology took from Aristotle,[29] which led to a static view of creation that Teilhard found unacceptable.

It is easy to see how neither of these notions of space or place are suitable for speaking of the relationship between God and place. Origen was the first to give theology a truly helpful view of place. Origen appropriated the Stoic principle that if something is to be comprehensible it must be limited. He understood that God cannot be comprehended by us. But what if we turn it around? What happens when God comprehends us and the cosmos? Then the cosmos becomes rational and comprehensible to us. In other words, while God may not be comprehended by us on this side of the cosmos, God in comprehending the cosmos sets up its limits and boundaries so that it becomes understandable to us.[30] Other Greek theologians understood Origen's achievement and offered variations. In essence, what Origen had offered was a relational view of place that neither Plato nor Aristotle had imagined. God made room for Godself so that we could have room for ourselves! In this Origen surpassed Plato, for he found a way in which the invisible and the visible would not be dualistically separated. Both the visible and the invisible found room in the place that God made for Godself in the cosmos.

Unfortunately, this marvelous insight of the Greek fathers soon became lost in the Latin West. As Aristotle's writings began to influence medieval theology, Aristotle's understanding of place as a bounded container began to play havoc with Christian understandings of place. The relational notion of place became forgotten, to be replaced by an absolute, infinitely extended notion of space. Casey blames it on the universalizing tendency of a Renaissance theology that got translated into globalizing modernity. Renaissance theology developed a doctrine of God that emphasized God's absolute power over and against God's ordaining power. God's absolute power may be referred to as the "poof" power of God. It is the power God has to "poof" creatures into being from absolutely nothing. God's ordaining power, on the other hand, is the power God has to create the world in the particular form that it has. It is an ordering power, the power of an artist.

A cosmos solely "poofed" into being, created solely by God's absolute power, knows nothing of connectedness. Each individual creature is solely defined by its existence. Only in a cosmos where God's ordaining power is at work can a creature know itself by its relationships to other creatures. This has unfortunate implications in the understanding of place. If one asks the question, Where is God?, the only answer possible in a world of individual, solitary existences is—God is everywhere. In other words, a God of absolute power can only be thought of in terms of an absolute, infinitely extended space. This absolute, infinitely extended space became the prime spatial orientation of the new sciences developing out of the work of Newton and Galileo.[31]

Foucault insightfully notes that "the real scandal of Galileo's work lay not so much in his discovery, or rediscovery, that the earth revolved around the sun, but in his constitution of an infinite and an infinitely open space."[32] Newton followed with his idea of absolute space and the new physics made the idea of absolute, infinite space victorious over place. Another way to put it is that the new natural science's view of space saw places as mere locations stripped of all relationality with finite human flesh, aspirations, memories, or stories. Yet the story of the diminishment of place does not end there.

The new natural sciences were ultimately concerned with motion. Galileo was interested in how fast cannonballs accelerated when dropped from a tower or the period of a pendulum as one shortened its string. Newton applied the new mathematics of calculus to predict the trajectory of a particle in motion. Yet studies of motion could not really progress until time could be measured. Absolute, infinitely extended space offered a means of measuring time. Space marked off in absolutely, discrete units can be used to count units of time. Think about a clock. What is a clock but time spatialized in discrete intervals? This meant that, for the new natural sciences, space was a means to an end, the measurement and theorizing of time. It also meant the subordination of space to time. In other words, the notion of place gave way to the notion of space that, in turn, became subordinated to the notion of time.[33]

The story, then, appears to be that of an unexamined collaboration between theology and science in the fifteenth and sixteenth century where a view of God's absolute power influenced the rise of the new natural sciences by giving them the notion of an absolute, infinitely extended space. This notion came about through the transformation of the relational notion of place to space and then to time. I believe theology left to itself would have eventually corrected the one-sided emphasis of God's absolute power in the doctrine of creation. Unfortunately, the success of the new natural sciences appears to have given this theological supposition the status of an infallible doctrine. It is no wonder, then, that place has had so little consideration in theology. The future has taken over front and center in contemporary theological cosmologies. Without place, however, there can be little room for speaking of heaven and earth, much less the visible and the invisible. Indeed, one of the casualties of this cosmological shift for theology was the weakening of its doctrine of the invisible.

A Place for the Invisible

Indeed, without the concept of place it is difficult to understand what theology means by the invisible. Perhaps Gaston Bachelard, the great Roman Catholic philosopher, can help theology reclaim the term. In his book, *The Poetics of Space*, Bachelard suggests that the invisible is revealed in the psychic or interiority of the human soul and, as such, it is intrinsically a place. Bachelard gave as example the poetic image. He claimed it was not the causal product of the mind. Its freshness and sudden appearance means the poetic image "has an entity and a dynamism of its own. It is directly referable to a direct *ontology*."[34] In other words, the poetic image comes before thought. Yet even more striking, poetic images exhibit a marvelous trans-subjectivity. The world without finds intimate space within the poetic imagination. As Bachelard put it,

> How can an image, at times very unusual, appear to be a concentration of the entire psyche? How—with no preparation—can this singular, short-lived event constituted by the appearance of an unusual poetic image, react on other minds and in other hearts, despite all the common barriers of common sense, all the disciplined schools of thought, content in their immobility?[35]

This means that poetic images are not phenomena of the mind, for the mind would have put obstacles to such transsubjectivity. No, poetic images, in their freshness yet transsubjectivity, are phenomena of the soul.

But what is this soul? Bachelard answers that it is an abode, "our first universe, a real cosmos in every sense of the word."[36] As such, it is the dwelling of a tremendous intimacy—indeed, an "intimate immensity."[37] Place, however, is all about intimacy. The poetic imagination works by giving poetic images space within the abode of this intimate immensity. When that happens "poetic spatiality . . . goes from deep intimacy to infinite extent."[38] It is capable of a marvelous transsubjectivity whereby the world outside the soul is able to become one with the place that is the soul. As Bachelard explains,

> It would seem, then, that it is through their "immensity" that these two kinds of space—the space of intimacy and the world space—blend. When human solitude deepens, then the two immensities touch and become identical. In one of Rilke's letters, we see him straining toward the "unlimited solitude that makes a lifetime of

each day, toward communion with the universe, in a word, space that the invisible space that man can live in nevertheless, and which surrounds him with countless presences."[39]

Bachelard helps us understand the topography of a theological cosmology. It must include the "within" of the cosmos as well as its "without." The "within" of the cosmos we grasp, as Pseudo-Dionysius saw so well, through poetic images. This "within" is an intimate immensity commensurate with the immensity of the "without" of the cosmos. It is also the place of the invisible. It is the place that is heaven and it abides in the human soul.

At Home in the Cosmos Again

Bachelard's *Poetics of Space* can help us ask whether we are at home in the cosmos in a new and profound way. To be at home in the cosmos it is necessary to make room for an intimate immensity, that is, the invisible. But what exactly does this mean? Here Teilhard can be quite helpful, because he has an implicit understanding of the invisible. Paradoxically, it is to be found in his doctrine of the visible.

Teilhard was profoundly visual.[40] At the very opening of *The Human Phenomenon* he tells us:

One could say that the whole of life lies in seeing—if ultimately, at least essentially. To be more is to be united—and this sums up and is the very conclusion of the work to follow. But unity grows, and we will affirm this again, only if it is supported by an increase of consciousness, of vision. That is probably why the history of the living world can be reduced to the elaboration of ever more perfect eyes at the heart of a cosmos where it is always possible to discern more. Are not the perfection of an animal and the supremacy of the thinking being measured by the penetration and power of synthesis of their glance?[41]

How Teilhard understands vision is remarkable. Vision is not a sensation but a kind of consciousness or, rather, a growth in consciousness. Moreover, it is a consciousness that supports the union with that which is seen! In Teilhard, vision is a sensibility to union, which, in turn, is a growth in being. So, in seeing, one also becomes united to what is seen.[42]

But what is seen? Teilhard answers: a divine milieu, a luminous world illuminated by Christ's transfiguring presence. This divine milieu is the place where we live and move and have our being and becoming, surrounded, penetrated, and shaped by Christ's divine loving presence.[43] Vision entails a sensibility to a fire glowing deep within the heart of matter. In catching sight of this fiery glow we are united to that which it illumines. Our vision unites us to this transfiguring milieu and, in doing so, we give shape to the evolving universe. Thus, what is seen as a divine transfiguring light illumining our world is the shaping of a new reality! As David Grumett puts it,

> The vision of the cosmos spiritually transfigured performs an analogous function for Teilhard to that of imagination in the Ignatian spiritual exercises, which creates *une logique de rupture et d'instauration historique*. The imagination does not simply receive images of reality passively, but employs spiritual images to construct that reality.[44]

As such, Teilhard's cosmology of vision lends itself to comparison with Bachelard's poetics of space. Just as Bachelard's poetic images create room in the soul, Teilhard's vision creates room in the cosmos. While Bachelard's treatment emphasizes interiority, Teilhard's emphasizes cosmology, albeit a cosmology that includes interiority. Furthermore, Teilhard's Christic transfiguring light is a restorative light, a healing light reconciling the cosmos and shepherding it to a new creation.

Together, Teilhard and Bachelard offer a topography of the invisible that is inextricably connected to the visible. In other words, the cosmos is a dynamic place where the invisible is being made visible. It is a place of reconciliation. Heaven and earth interpenetrate thanks to the transfiguring light of Christ present at the heart of matter but also due to those who in seeing the light transform themselves and the world by their vision.

This is, then, a dynamic view of being at home in the cosmos. It is an eschatological view. We are home already and not yet. Christ offers the cosmos to us again as place where we can experience an "intimate immensity." It must be done, however, through an imagination akin to poetic imagery, imagery that creates room—room for light, and life, and, Teilhard would add, fire. But how does this imagination work itself out practically into reality? And will it result in the kind of place we can call home? Indeed, what exactly is home?

What Is Home?

The question of the place called home is an important one to theological cosmology. Our answer involves how we understand our relationship to the cosmos, our responsibilities to our shaping of this relationship, and, more profoundly, our own understanding of what it means to be human. To address these issues, we must tackle an aspect of our humanity that attempts to reach heaven from the earth. I am speaking of the biblical dialectic exemplified in the story of the Tower of Babel. In the Bible, the Tower of Babel signifies a profound reflection of humanity's true home. Is our true home in the city or in the garden? The dialectic begins at the beginning, that is, in the book of Genesis.

Anyone reading the first few pages of Genesis will notice that there are two accounts of creation.[45] The first one sees the human in his and her glory. They are at home in the cosmos. In fact, they are told to "be fruitful and multiply, and fill the earth and subdue it; and have dominion over the fish of the sea and over the birds of the air and over every living thing that moves upon the earth" (Gen. 1:28). The second sees the human in their tragedy. Born at home in the cosmos, they now must struggle to survive in the cosmos. The human is told, ". . . Cursed is the ground because of you; in toil you shall eat of it all the days of your life; thorns and thistles it shall bring forth for you; and you shall eat the plants of the field. By the sweat of your face you shall eat bread until you return to the ground, for out of it you were taken; you are dust, and to dust you shall return" (Gen. 2:17-19).

The striking difference between the accounts is not that in one the human is destined to build glorious cities and in the other one must scratch out a living from the ground. Rather, the difference lies in the nature of human engagement with the cosmos. In one, the engagement is glorious; in the other, it is struggle. This curious mix of glory and struggle points to a great mystery not only about our humanity but also about our cosmos. The cosmos is our home but it is so only if we learn how to live in it. In other words, the human must come to know the inner and outer workings of the cosmos if he and she are to find life within the cosmos. This call to cosmic knowledge surely must be part of the mystery that is human. It is also a mystery about the cosmos. It calls us to be known.

But the mystery lies deeper than merely a call to know and be known. The depth of the mystery lies in the nature of the call. That call is a mix of effortless dominion and an innocence to be regained. How we as humans come to know the cosmos is as important to our survival as the knowing of the cosmos itself. It asks for a kind of knowing that gives mastery in a graceful and effortless way yet somehow makes us innocent toward the cosmos again.

The Tower of Babel could have been a vision of salvation, of bringing heaven and earth together again. It turned out, however, to be a commentary on the nature of the sin of Adam and Eve. Knowledge that leads to arrogance brings forth a dominion that further separates heaven and earth. If the expulsion from the garden signifies anything, it is that human striving becomes salvific when it leads to an innocence regained. It is a knowing that involves sacrifice but in the learning a new innocence is regained that leads to an effortless living in the cosmos again.

The character Malcolm in Michael Crichton's best-selling novel *Jurassic Park* could have been talking about the Tower of Babel as he judges the genetic engineering that is the subject of the novel:

> "I'll tell you what I'm talking about," he said. "Most kinds of power require a substantial sacrifice by whoever wants the power. There is an apprenticeship, a discipline lasting many years. Whatever kind of power you want. President of the company. Black belt in karate. Spiritual guru. Whatever it is you seek, you have to put in the time, the practice, the effort. You must give up a lot to get it. It has to be very important to you. And once you have attained it, it is your power. It can't be given away: it resides in you. It is literally the result of your discipline . . . that kind of power has a built-in control. The discipline of getting the power changes you so that you won't abuse it. . . . But scientific power is like inherited wealth. You read what others have done and you take the next step. You can do it very young. You make progress very fast. There is no discipline lasting many decades. There is no mastery: old scientists are ignored. There is no humility before nature. . . . You don't even know exactly what you have done but you have reported it, patented it, and sold it. And the buyer will have even less discipline than you. The buyer simply purchases the power like any commodity. The buyer doesn't even conceive that any discipline might be necessary."[46]

Malcolm, I believe, reveals the tension between the city and the garden for us today It is what we call technology. As such, technology lies at the heart of what home means, that is, home in the cosmos.[47] Malcolm sees our home in the cosmos as shaped by a power gained by a kind of disciplined knowing of the cosmos as home, a discipline that leads to humility before nature. It is a discipline that sees power not as a means of selling and buying a commodity but in preparing to receive and to give back a gift. Our home in the cosmos is not a commodity but a gift. But what sort of discipline can help technology make a home in the cosmos?

In his insightful book, *Technology and Human Becoming,* my dear friend and mentor Philip Hefner suggests that the human process of becoming is unavoidably technological. Hefner, in fact, sees technology as "being about being finite, frail, and mortal. Technology is also about being free and imagining things and conditions that never were, things that do not exist, and conditions that can be different."[48] As such, technology lies more in the spiritual realm than in the business realm. Here Hefner agrees with the psychologist Mihaly Csikszentmihaly's understanding of spirituality. Spirituality is the place where our imaginings make us sensible to "possibilities which our material world is not sensitive to."[49] The imaginative spirit, Hefner believes, is the heart of human spirituality. And freedom is the heart of the imagination. As such, technology requires discipline, the discipline appropriate to the freedom that is our imagination. But how does one discipline freedom?

Here one must understand the conditions of human freedom. It is not like God's. It is finite, frail, and vulnerable. Hefner puts it succinctly: "Freedom to be. Freedom to imagine, and vulnerability—they all go together."[50] A disciplined freedom is the condition of the spiritual. It is the door to our home in the cosmos. Thus, the importance to the following questions: What sort of discipline is it? What keeps us from using our imagination foolishly? What keeps us from commodifying the very home we must build? What sort of imagination makes a gift of cosmic knowledge?

Perhaps an answer can be found in a little known book by Lewis Hyde called *The Gift*, where the author asks a surprisingly fertile question: "Why do we suspect that Silhouette Romances will not be enduring works of art? What is it about a work, even when it is bought and sold in the market, that makes us distinguish it from such pure commodities as these?"[51] The question is fertile because an answer to his question is also an answer to a variety of other profound questions that involve the nature of gift. His answer is striking. "That art that matters to us—which moves the heart, or revives the soul, or delights the senses, or offers courage for living, however we choose to describe the experience—that work is received by us as a gift is received."[52]

Hyde goes on to make a striking observation. Gift has two senses: an inner and an outer sense. The inner sense of gift is the sense of being gifted, of being given a talent or charism. The outer sense of gift is the sense of gift as vehicle of culture, of that which creates relationships based on the reception of a gift. Both these senses are demonstrated in the marvelous fairy tale of the elves and the shoemaker as told by Hyde.

> A shoemaker is down on his luck and has only enough leather to sew a single pair of shoes. He cuts the leather out and goes to bed, planning to sew the shoes in the morning. During the night, two naked elves come and make the shoes. The shoemaker is speechless with astonishment when he finds them. Not a stitch is out of place! The shoes are such a masterpiece that the first customer to appear in the morning pays handsomely for them, and the cobbler has enough money to buy leather for two pairs of shoes. That night he cuts the leather out and goes to bed. Again in the morning the shoes are made, and again they sell for such a price as to afford the leather for four pairs of shoes. In this way the shoemaker soon

prospers. One evening, not long before Christmas, the cobbler suggests to his wife that they stay up and see who has been helping them. They leave a candle burning, hide behind some coats, and, at midnight, see the elves come in and set to work. In the morning the wife says to the shoemaker, "The little men have made us rich and we should show our gratitude for this. They are running about with nothing on and might freeze! I will make them each a shirt, coat, jacket, trousers and a pair of stockings. Why don't you make them each a pair of little shoes?" The cobbler willingly agrees, and one night when the clothes are finished, he lays them out on the bench in place of the leather. He and his wife hide behind the coats to watch. The elves are surprised and pleased to find the clothes. They put them on and sing "We're sleek, we're fine, we're out the door. We shan't be cobblers anymore!" and they dance around the room and away. They never return, but everything continues to go well with the shoemaker and he prospers at whatever he takes in hand.[53]

Hyde sees this story as the parable of a gifted person. It describes the process by which the stirrings of a gift, that is, the potential of a gift, goes on and becomes an actual gift. That process entails our attending to the gift initially at work in us. There is a reciprocity of labor, a labor of gratitude, between gift and recipient that progresses toward a spiritual transformation. The shoemaker, for example, finally decides to stay awake and watch at night. With what he learns he makes a new gift, shoes for the elves, but he does it as a gifted man. What was gift now becomes giver.

As Hyde explains,

Between the time a gift comes to us and the time we pass it along, we suffer gratitude. Moreover, with gifts that are agents of change, it is only when the gift has worked in us, only when we have come up to its level, as it were, that we can give it away again. Passing the gift along is the act of gratitude that finishes the labor. The transformation is not accomplished until we have the power to give the gift on our own terms. Therefore, the end of the labor of gratitude is similarity with the gift or with its donor. Once this similarity has been achieved we may feel a lingering and generalized gratitude, but we won't feel it with the urgency of true indebtedness.

I believe this is the kind of discipline to which the *Jurassic Park* character Malcolm refers and the kind of imagination for which Hefner calls. Let me suggest that Hyde's understanding of gift offers us the kind of imagination for the sort of technology with which we who are human must build a home for ourselves in the cosmos.

As such, it is a very different kind of technology from what Silicon Valley now offers us. It is a technology that promotes communities of gratitude not consumerism, vulnerability not invincibility, a graceful mastery that gives not an oppressive dominion that kills. It is a technology associated with the arts. It is a way of life in the ways of beauty. For this is the spiritual dimension of beauty, that it is gift. For this reason, we must add a new dimension to our cosmology: it is not only a place but it is a place of beauty.

4

Endless Forms Most Beautiful[1]

Darwin is not usually thought of as a poet but there is an often-quoted passage in the first edition of his *The Origin of Species* that is as breathtaking as any that Gerard Manley Hopkins might have written:

> There is a grandeur in this view of life, with its several powers, having been originally breathed into a few forms or into one: and that whilst this planet has gone cycling on according to the fixed law of gravity, *from so simple a beginning endless forms most beautiful have been, and are being, evolved.*[2]

As one ponders the many debates surrounding the issues that evolutionary theory raises, it is puzzling that Darwin's observation has been given little, if any, consideration. Perhaps part of the reason is that these debates have focused on the nature and role of efficient natural causes rather than on the nature and role of natural forms.

Beauty in the Living World

The time has come to address a missing piece in the debate, namely the significance of beautiful forms in an evolutionary world. Focusing on form rather than efficient cause gives us an effective framework to understand the significance of evolutionary theory, as well as a powerful guide in articulating a theology of evolution. Moreover, by focusing on form—that is, beautiful form—the deep principles that underlie the unity and diversity of life become apparent in a way that not only satisfies the mind but also the heart. Finally, the endless beautiful forms of nature provide a key to discovering humanity's home in the cosmos.

Why Beautiful Form?

Form is a notion that draws suspicion in science. It is a notion that has ancient and powerful philosophical roots. Form conjures up twin evils to those who are convinced that nature is self-referential, i.e., that natural knowledge has no other reference but to other natural knowledge. These twin evils are *telos* and mindfulness.[3] For this reason, if not for any other, form has faded as a natural explanation and cause (i.e., efficient cause) has risen as the major category for scientific explanation of natural reality.[4] But can efficient cause adequately account for evolutionary process? As Ernst Mayr and others have pointed out the field of biology has telic dimensions.[5] When one deals with living realities, *telos* is a characteristic that must be faced in any scientific account. Yet *telos* implies design, and design implies a mind. If it is not God or a human mind behind such *telos*, then who is? Is it possible that nature herself designs? Can we ask of nature who it is, not merely what does it do?

The question becomes relevant when addressing natural human reality. While many hesitate to acknowledge it, mindfulness and design do exist in nature. The creature writing this book is evidence of that. At this point a stubborn dualism reveals itself in the struggle to catch an overall view of the natural world. Mind is thought to be somehow different than nature. Nature, in such dualism, eschews mindfulness. Yet, unless one is willing to separate the human reality from natural reality, one cannot avoid the inescapable: living, natural reality exhibits both telic and mind-like processes. These aspects of natural reality are best understood through the category of form. Indeed, let me be bold enough to suggest that evolutionary theory itself demands an understanding of form.

Into the Cool: An Expanded Understanding of Matter

What makes form rather than efficient cause a better candidate to understand evolutionary process? The findings of a new field in physics offer an answer. In 1971, Eric Schneider asked two particularly fertile questions about the nature of casuality in holistic natural systems such as an ecosystem.[6] Do laws exist that govern the behavior of whole ecosystems? If so, what are they?[7] Ecosystems are defined by their holistic structure. It does no good to understand an ecosystem solely by its parts; understanding one requires understanding the whole. This seems counter to scientific investigation that works by looking at the parts rather than the whole. Yet there is a characteristic of a holistic system that lends itself to scientific analysis. A holistic system becomes whole by means of a boundary that separates an interior from an exterior. But the interior and exterior are not closed off from one another; rather, they are constantly exchanging energy. Such a system is said to be an open system or a system in nonequilibrium.

In a nonequilibrium system, the boundary between the interior and its exterior constitutes what scientists call a gradient. A gradient is nothing more than a change, gradual or abrupt, in temperature (or density, potential—indeed, almost any physical property) from a higher to a lower intensity, from hot to cool. It is the gradient that allows energy exchange to occur between the interior and exterior.[8] The field of nonequilibrium thermodynamics has been studying the properties of gradients in open systems for many years. Its findings are remarkable. Nature does, indeed, abhor a gradient. And it does so by attempting to collapse the gradient by generating spontaneous and growing complex systems characterized by stunning, beautiful forms. Nature tends to flow into the cool and it does so beautifully.

Nonequilibrium thermodynamics brings the relevance of form to our understanding of nature. This ought not to surprise us. Form, after all, best describes holistic systems such as the one found in such nonequilibrium phenomena as living creatures. Yet nonequilibrium thermodynamics does not offer us the typical notion of form such as found in classical philosophy or art theory. Nonequilibrium form, or living form, is form arising out of and defining an open system, that is, a system in which energy flows in and out.

In other words, living form is form in flux. An example might be a candle flame. A flame has characteristics of classical form but it differs from classic form by its dynamism. It is form characterized by a stable structure that owes its structure to a stable process in an inherently unstable system. Being part of an open system means that such form is at the same time permanent and changeable; it can grow and shrink yet has discernible integrity and coherence of shape or arrangement. Living form is form, but it is form that cannot be pinned down in any absolute way. It is form that is contingent, dynamic, and even kenotic. It is form with which a theologian can live.

Living form, moreover, has striking parallels to artistic form. Artistic form arises out of modeling previous forms. Living form, arising out of nonequilibrium thermodynamics, also follows such modeling. As Schneider and Sagan put it:

The evolution of the chromosomes-containing nucleated cell that looks more or less like an amoeba on its own, and which forms the basis for all plants, animals, and fungi, did not appear from scratch: it is the result of bacteria with distinct metabolic abilities that devoured and infected each other. Organisms are not put together atom by atom, molecule by molecule, but modularly, a genome at a time. Once we realize that organisms tend to evolve like an artist sampling pre-existing works—once we realize that there is more to evolution that single mutations—the chances of a given life-form such as a praying mantis or a slime mold evolving seem less in need of divine intervention.[9]

Nonequilibrium thermodynamics seems to give scientific weight to Darwin's poetic insight: "From so simple a beginning, endless forms most beautiful have been, and are being, evolved." The artistry of natural forms does not by itself speak of divine intervention, as Schneider is quick to point out. On the other hand, Schneider and Sagan do not go far enough in pointing out that when form is introduced in natural explanations it is tantamount to changing a long-reigning scientific paradigm which focuses on efficient cause.

For me, however, the more important question that Schneider and Sagan do not consider concerns the beauty of such forms. Are the forms of nonequilibrium thermodynamics beautiful? I am arguing that they are. Yet their beauty is not to be found in the sense of an Enlightenment aesthetics, that is, as a disinterested judgment of taste, but in a more profound way, a way deeply embedded in nature herself.[10] Schneider and Sagan, for example, comment on the forms created when a liquid is heated and rotated at the same time. These forms are known as Bénard cells, which form beautiful spiral, polygonal patterns in the liquid:

No adequate theory exists to explain the patterns. Yet we are sure that these exquisite spirals and targets occur in a specific solution of sulfur hexafluoride that organizes in response to a thermal gradient. . . . The complex organization that attacks the gradient is not just pretty. It has a form and a function. This marriage of aesthetics and utility is no invention of architects or visible deities. Rather, its roots are in nonliving processes in a world of energy.[11]

What the observation by Schneider and Sagan suggests is that both classical and modern understandings of beautiful form need revision. There is a sense of beauty found in the complexity and diversity of natural evolutionary forms that has no exact equivalent in the history of philosophy or aesthetics.

Toward a New Understanding of Form

A new understanding of form may begin by asking the seemingly simple question: What does evolutionary theory know? Or, another way to ask the same question, What is the subject of evolutionary theory? In other words, what is the *what* of evolutionary theory? This question has been, in the main, ignored simply because much of the discussion on evolution has focused on the *how* rather than on the *what* of evolutionary theory.

This question of the *what* of evolutionary theory, however, is not easy to answer, for one must address not only the *accuracy* of the answer but also its *adequacy*. To say, for instance, that the subject of evolutionary theory is the variation of species or of populations of living organisms may serve the issue of accuracy but not of adequacy. This is because evolutionary theory has become the central principle of the discipline of biology itself. The *what* of evolutionary theory, in other words, has become the *what* of the discipline of biology. This raises deep issues for biology as a discipline that have not been adequately addressed.

For example, the traditional *what* of biology has been nothing less than life itself. A complication sets in, however, because to have life as the subject of a question poses issues that are best articulated as *why* questions. In other words, there is an intrinsic and inextricable connection between the *what* of biology and the *why* of life. Contemporary biology has avoided this connection by avoiding the *what* question. This is understandable, for if the *what* of evolution has something to do with the *why* of life, then one risks introducing a second principle besides matter into biological thought. The belief that a second principle is needed in nature to explain life is called vitalism. It seems undeniable that the nature of life is different from the nature of matter. Similarly, it also seems undeniable that the *how* of life is different from the *how* of matter.

Nevertheless, biologists are suspicious of any approach that smacks of such dualism. Matter and life are observed to be intrinsically connected in a way that defies dualistic explanations. On the other hand, monistic answers cannot explain the difference between living matter and dead material. The lack of an adequate metaphysics that is neither monistic or dualistic may be the reason why biologists have avoided asking about the *what* of their discipline.

Such questions cannot continue to be avoided. The *what* of evolutionary theory is particularly crucial for biology, as it goes to the root intelligibility of the discipline. For while it is clear that the dynamism of life necessarily must be understood as continuous with the dynamism of the material in the universe; it is also clear that such understanding is not sufficient. More important, is the growing realization that all living creatures are mediated, i.e., interrelated. A living creature supports other living creatures and, in turn, it is supported by them. Such mediation can only take place if there is a *what* to interrelate or mediate.[12] If vitalism is excluded, and if material explanations are necessary but insufficient, then life must be understood as a challenge to our understanding of matter, or our understanding of matter has to be radically expanded.

This problematic is expressed in the question, What does biology study? Biologists usually answer that they study living processes, not life itself. While living processes are a necessary focus of biology, they are not sufficient, for it turns the subject of biology into an adjective as opposed to a noun.[13] In other words, a typical biologist might feel comfortable speaking of a living virus or a living plant but not of a virus life or a plant life. The exclusive study of how an organism maintains itself, reproduces, develops, and changes in time, avoids vitalism but also limits our language about life to an adjective. While such language is necessary, it is not sufficient. It makes equal sense to speak of a plant life or a virus life as to speak of a living plant or a living virus. It is this dual aspect of life, life as noun and adjective, that makes it such an affront to contemporary thought. Life cannot be understood in monistic terms or in dualist terms, because our cosmos itself cannot be explained in either of these terms. There is a dimension to the cosmos beyond space and time, namely, depth. Life, of all phenomena, is best described in terms of depth.

What is this depth that characterizes life? As a first approximation, let's look at life as a noun. To ask this is to ask the question of what makes a living creature be that which it is; that is, What is its form? However, to ask this question is to recognize what is known as formal causality, a causality that is different from those that make machines run. Formal causality explains the activity of the whole as a whole. It is the principle by which the many possibilities of molecules and cell parts and cells become this particular living whole. Formal causality does not force an effect but, rather, is the unifying principle that brings the many possibilities of parts into a living whole. It is causality from the "inside out" as opposed to the "bottom up."[14] In other words, it is an immanent causality. It is form emerging from the deep.[15]

Life as an adjective does not fit well with the nature of form, however. Life as an adjective implies a dynamism that qualifies a noun. When applied to form it appears we have an oxymoron. Dynamic form refers both to a stable structure and a stable process. In other words, living form may be seen as a shape in time. Living forms have a beginning, a middle, and an end.[16]

Yet this is not enough. For living forms are more than dynamic forms. They are more than nouns that are also adjectives. For living form is also radically interconnected with other forms. If biology has given humanity a true gift in understanding, it is this. Life is an entangled web of living forms based on yet-to-be-understood processes of life and death. One living form, in dying, leads to other forms becoming alive. Forms do not merely die, they make possible other forms in their dying. This is what I mean in suggesting that natural living forms are kenotic. In their self-emptying, they bring forth new life. In other words, living forms are not only shapes of time; they are also places for time. Kenotic living forms create a place where time takes shape. Here we enter the true dimension of depth. Living forms create a place deep in space and time. In this depth, a cosmic story is being told. This story is not the same as a human story for it also includes the human itself as part of the story. These cosmic stories found in the deep of living forms tell a tale only heard by those who are willing to open themselves up to the depth dimension of the universe. Nowhere is this clearer than in the growing field of evolutionary developmental biology.

The Entangled Bank

Charles Darwin, in a letter to Asa Gray, wrote in 1860 that "embryology is to me by far the strongest single class of facts in favor of change of forms, and not one, I think, of my reviewers has alluded to this."[17] Darwin's complaint is echoed today in the way the scientific study of form has been neglected in the debate over evolutionary theory. It is gratifying, then, to see how embryology is now becoming an exciting field of discovery. In its study of the shape and the way living form develops it is contributing to our understanding both of life and of evolution.

What is the science of developing forms such as found in embryology and developmental biology contributing to evolutionary theory? First, it is providing answers to questions that the "Modern Synthesis," as the standard form of evolutionary theory is called, could not and would not face. As Sean Carroll describes it:

> The Modern Synthesis established much of the foundation for how evolutionary biology has been discussed and taught for the past sixty years. However, despite the monikers of "Modern" and "Synthesis," it was incomplete. At the time of its formulation and until recently, we could say that forms do change, and that natural selection is a force, but we could say nothing about *how* forms change, about the visible drama of evolution as depicted, for example, in the fossil record. The Synthesis treated embryology as a "black box" that somehow transformed genetic information into three-dimensional, functional animals.[18]

A scientific view such as the Modern Synthesis revealed its preoccupation with efficient causes and its neglect of form in scientific explanation. In this view, genes are the efficient cause of evolutionary forms. The forms themselves, at best, are to be appreciated; at worst, to be seen as irrelevant.

Into this came a dedicated group of scientists who began to study the genes responsible for fruit fly development. Their study found a marvelous order and logic that underlay not only the generation of the fruit fly form but all animal form. Their studies

> revealed that despite their great differences and physiology, all complex animals—flies and flycatchers, dinosaurs and tribolites,

butterflies and zebras and humans—share a common "tool kit" of "master" genes that govern the formation and patterning of their bodies and body parts. . . . We now know from sequencing the entire DNA of species (their *genomes*) that not only do flies and humans share a large cohort of developmental genes, but that mice and humans have virtually identical sets of about 29,000 genes, and that chimps and humans are nearly 99 percent identical at the DNA level.[19]

What Carroll's description of his field of developmental evolutionary biology ought to tell us is that wherever "black boxes" exist in scientific theory, what may be found inside them is even more stunning, indeed beautiful, scientific theory.

The second lesson we ought to learn from developmental environmental biology is that form cannot be seen as an ancillary category in scientific explanation. Indeed, "the evolution of form is the main drama of life's story, both as found in the fossil record and in the diversity of living species."[20] But perhaps the greatest gift of evolutionary developmental biology, indeed of evolutionary theory in general, is the possibility of a new understanding of form that can give us a new understanding and appreciation of beauty and the profound aesthetic roots of natural reality.

Darwin best articulated this new understanding of form that is deeply rooted, so to speak, in the soil of nature through his description of the "entangled bank" in *The Origin of Species*:

It is interesting to contemplate an entangled bank, clothed with many plants of many kinds, with birds singing on the bushes, with various insects flitting bout, and with worms crawling through the damp earth, and to reflect that these elaborately constructed forms, so different from each other, and dependent on each other in so complex a manner, have all been produced by laws acting around us.[21]

What Darwin astutely noted is that living form must be understood not only in the singular but, above all, in the plural. Living form or, rather, natural form is characterized by an interdependent dimension, namely, that natural form cannot be thought of apart from natural forms. It is this interdependent relationship of form to forms that characterizes natural complexity.

As such, natural complexity is ill served by the notion of an emergent, irreducible whole. It is the plurality of forms in a special kind of unity that together describes nature's complexity. While such unity leads to a whole, this unity is not the whole itself. If it were then there would be no real significance to the parts that make the whole. No, the unity is more subtle and profound. It is the unity that binds the parts and the whole.

As such, it is a unity that has its basis in the kenosis of contingency. The self-giving of life to create more life consists of forms existing as stable but fragile structures intertwined with stable but fragile processes. Furthermore, these forms give rise and intertwine with other forms in a great dynamism of forms in such a way that each form is dynamically dependent on the other. This dynamic dependence makes for a dynamic unity that is strikingly beautiful both in its parts and as a whole. This contingent, delicate, and fragile dynamic unity within diversity corresponds almost exactly to a 2,500-year-old consensus regarding beauty. Beauty is a unity in diversity.[22]

The "entangled bank" view of beauty, however, adds two other elements to the beautiful. The beautiful in nature not only is a deep unity of a marvelous diversity of form but also is a deep unity of an endless and contingent variety of forms. In other words, it is a place where time takes shape and form in the kenotic self-emptying of life unto life. Thus, forms as shapes of time and as kenotic are two elements of beautiful form not found in the classical account. As such, it reveals a reality whose complexity cannot be described simply as an emergent, irreducible whole. Neither can such complex reality be described as a chaotic plurality of forms. Rather, the complex reality that is life can only be described as beautiful in the sense of a profound unity within contingent, kenotic forms creating a place for and endlessly giving shape to time.

But what is this place where time is shaped with living form? It is a place of wondrous tales, of a cosmic story being whispered from the depth of the entangled, living web of dynamic forms. It is a tale complete with verbs, noun, and adjectives punctuated by the drama of kenotic life, life emptying itself to death, which then gives rise to life again. The theologian cannot help but see in this story the eternal music coming out of the divine life itself, the dynamics of the paschal mystery heard through the strings of living, dynamic forms. Out of the deep of the cosmos living forms as shapes of time weave a cosmic story played as a cosmic song heard only by those who allow their hearts to be moved by their music and their tale. Indeed, beauty is the depth dimension of the cosmos. And to experience beauty is to know we are swimming in the cosmic deep.

Beauty and the Deep

I believe Teilhard knew beauty to be the manifestation of the cosmic deep. As I argued earlier, his mystical experiences were aesthetic experiences of the divine, based on associating beauty and the deep. In his mystical visions, he entered into the heart of matter through the experience of "the light and colors of beauties" of the cosmos. As he entered their depths he found the source of their beauty in "the incommunicable Beauty of Christ." Teilhard's visions found beauty as the source of the deep. But did Teilhard do justice to this association? For the "incommunicable beauty" of Christ is inextricable from the beauty of all three persons of the one divine life. The deep that Teilhard found in the beauty of Christ's transfiguring light is nothing less than the trinitarian deep. In this, the theological tradition is clear. Divine beauty belongs to all persons of the Trinity but each person brings a different dimension to this beauty. More important, there is a long tradition that attributes the beauty of the cosmos to the work of the Holy Spirit.[23]

In his silence about the trinitarian basis of depth and beauty, Teilhard perhaps follows Bonaventure, who attributes beauty to the word that is the splendor of the eternal light.[24] We saw, after all, that Teilhard's aesthetics are strikingly similar to Bonaventure's. Yet Bonaventure's association of beauty with the word should not be taken as proposing an exclusive association. Let me suggest that this may be the reason why Teilhard lacks a theology of the Holy Spirit. Without a role for the Holy Spirit in the divine milieu, however, Teilhard's marvelous insights may go theologically awry. Most problematic is the role of sanctification and its relationship to salvation in Teilhard's system. Is sanctification part of the human phenomenon? Are we sanctified as we evolve or do we evolve because we are sanctified? Also, what is the relationship of sanctification to salvation in an evolving cosmos? Are we saved simply by evolving? Or must we sanctify our evolving to be saved? These questions are some of the most troubling in Teilhard's vision. They are questions that cry out for a theology of the Holy Spirit.

These questions alert us that a place for the Holy Spirit is crucial in a theological cosmology. If Christ's ascension to heaven makes a theological cosmology imperative, then the Holy Spirit, in making Christ present on earth, makes a theological cosmology possible. For it is the Holy Spirit that reveals and connects heaven and earth. This is the subject of sanctification and it is the key to finding our home in the cosmos. Teilhard may have failed in making this necessary connection but, in his aesthetics, he also gave us the means to help make the connection. The beautiful forms of the cosmos reveal the depths of the cosmos out of which the meaning of the struggle that is life is to be found. In this lies a nascent theology of the Holy Spirit on which a theological cosmology can be built.

For this reason, let us look at the tradition on divine beauty and the Spirit's role. It may be no surprise that here the Eastern and Western traditions differ. Patrick Sherry, in his book *Spirit and Beauty*, gives the main characteristics of an Eastern model:

> [The Eastern model] predicates beauty of all three Persons, but in different ways according to their roles in the Trinity: The Father is the source of Beauty, the Son is the perfect image or replica of the Father and radiates his glory (cf. Col. 1:15; Heb. 1:3; 2 Cor. 4:6) and the Spirit eternally manifests this glory and reflects the image in the world by completing and communicating divine revelation and by creating beauty and thus is, as it were, the 'point of contact' of the Trinity for us.[25]

The Western model, on the other hand, follows Augustine in seeing the Holy Spirit as the bond of love between Father and Son. Thus, the Spirit is the harmony of the Trinity and the locus of divine beauty, which overflows into the world.

Beauty, Form, and the Spirit

Hans Urs von Balthasar's rich and complex theological aesthetics takes both models to heart yet also gives a real advance in connecting beauty and the Spirit. Von Balthasar is interested in the peculiar knowing of faith. Faith, after all, is knowing both in an intellectual sense but also in a unitive sense. Faith knows both by grasping intellectually the truth of what it knows but also by becoming united to that which it knows. In Spanish, the words *saber* and *conocer* express this dual sense of knowing. In the technical language of medieval philosophy, these two kinds of knowing were signified by the words *species* and *lumen*.

Species has to do with the Aristotelian notion of substantial form. It is the deepest truth of a form as it is grasped by the intellect. Lumen has to do with the Augustinian notion of illumination. It refers to the deepest truth of a form grasped in the very experience of the goodness radiating from within the form. Von Balthasar saw these two ways to experience form as creating a needless dualism that can only be corrected by an aesthetics, the beautiful form. As he puts it,

> Each of these approaches grasps but one side of Christian faith, and of the insight and vision which belongs to it. For the first of these, insight rests on the evidential force of the credibility of the signs of revelation, which demand and elicit the act of faith. . . . For the second approach, insight rests essentially on the foundations of faith itself: faith perceives God's light, mediated, to be sure, by signs and witnesses, and yet even now with that secret immediacy which will one day emerge openly in the eternal vision.[26]

But

> with both these ways we still remain within a parallelism of ostensive sign and signified interior light. This dualism can be abolished only by introducing as well the thought-forms and categories of the beautiful. The beautiful is above all a form, and the light does not fall on this form from above and from outside, rather it breaks forth from the form's interior. . . . Visible form not only "points" to an invisible, unfathomable mystery; form is the apparition of this mystery, and reveals it while, naturally, at the same time protecting and veiling it. Both natural and artistic form has an exterior which appears and an interior depth, both of which, however, are not separable in the form itself. The content (*Gehalt*) does not lie behind the form (*Gestalt*), but within it. Whoever is not capable of seeing and "reading" the form will, by the same token, fail to perceive the content. Whoever is not illumined by the form will see no light in the content either.[27]

As we can see, in von Balthasar beautiful form encompasses the truth and goodness of that which is seen. Seeing beautiful form, however, is not automatic. One must be able to grasp or "read" the form as well as be illumined by it. This double aspect of faith, receptive illumination but also active reading of form, is what von Balthasar calls "seeing" the form.

Using the analogy of faith von Balthasar gives us a metaphysical basis for form. But this is not enough, for faith is more than being able to see the the truth, goodness, and beauty of the world; it is also how we come to know and love God. A metaphysics of form is not enough, it also requires a theology of form. For von Balthasar this means finding the basis of all forms. It is the Son who is The Form, that is, the model of all earthly forms. Thus, beautiful form is not only a matter of "seeing" a form but also a matter of "seeing The Form."

It is striking how this theology of form comes close to describing Teilhard's vision of the "lovely beauties" of the universe giving way to the "incommunicable Beauty of Christ." It should not surprise us, however, for in proposing a "within" and a "without" to all matter, Teilhard established the very conditions of form. More important, in seeing that all matter is illumined by the transfiguring light of Christ, Teilhard also gave us an example of von Balthasar's "seeing The Form." Von Balthasar, however, opens up a space for the Holy Spirit in his "seeing The Form" in the beautiful forms of the cosmos.

Von Balthasar draws on Origen to make an interesting observation. How can it be that the word that became flesh in the historical Jesus is also now for us the word but in the reality of the ascended Jesus? His answer reveals a powerful theology of the Holy Spirit. Since the Holy Spirit makes present Christ on earth and is the source and giver of life, then the word is also a living word, a word of life that also gives life. It is. As such, the Spirit is not the Word, and yet it is also the Spirit of the Word. But it does not proceed only from the Word but, simultaneously, also from the Father (Jn 15.26), who is God 'before the word.' He is at once the Spirit of the Utterable and the Unutterable. He explains the Word by showing it as it proceeds from what is eternally beyond the Word. He transfigures both realities in their unity, since he is the unity of both and witnesses to this fact. Thus, he is at once the Spirit of form and formation and a Spirit of love and enthusiasm. In this incomprehensible unity he is the locus of the beauty of God. He is sober to show forth very precisely what is and to allow it to be seen; and he is intoxication and intoxicates because the raptures of love are the ultimate objectivity which must be seen and experienced.[28]

Von Balthasar has in this profound paragraph given us a model that bridges both Eastern and Western models of trinitarian beauty. There is also in this paragraph much that von Balthasar suggests but, alas, does not develop.

Informed and In-Formed

If the Spirit is both the Spirit of form and formation as well as the locus of divine beauty, then we have a way to relate beautiful, living, dynamic form, form as noun and adjective, to God's ordaining power. The endless forms, which are most beautiful of cosmic evolution, do not merely evolve. Their beauty is both a sign and a locus for an encounter of God's ordaining love. In their kenotic dynamism of beauty, the entangled bank of living, beautiful forms make present Christ in his fully cosmic dimension. By fully cosmic I mean Christ made present in the cosmos through the action of the Holy Spirit. The fully cosmic dimension of Christ is revealed in the beauty of endless living natural forms. This is only possible through the Holy Spirit who makes Christ in heaven also present on earth.

In other words, the fully cosmic Christ is also the Christ who sends the Holy Spirit. More important, Christ in his fully cosmic dimensions shows us that to be fully human is to be at home in the cosmos. For the Holy Spirit is not only the ultimate source of the beauty of living forms but also the One who unites us to their beauty. In uniting us, the Holy Spirit shows us the way to our home in the cosmos. In other words, we are not simply to enjoy the beauty of living forms, we are also to be formed by their beauty. We are not simply to be informed by beautiful form but also in-formed.[29] This "in-formation" informed by the beauty of living, dynamic forms is the place that is our home in the cosmos, a home made possible through the grace of the Holy Spirit.

So what is this in-formed place? Like Bachelard's poetic imagination, it is a spiritual place. But it is more than that as well. It is a place made possible through the living matter that is beautiful dynamic form and, thus, it is a living form itself. It is an embodied place. As such, it has shape and spirit, story and openness, structure and dynamism, matter and life. Yet it is more, for it has come to be an embodied, spiritual place precisely through the grace of the Holy Spirit. As such, it is a place of abundance, a place of life abundant. By life abundant, I mean something akin to what scholastic theologians called the supernatural.[30] It is gifted givenness, that is, graced nature.

In other words, this in-formed place concerns the theological locus known as nature and grace. In a theological cosmology, the discussion that attempts to relate nature and grace takes a cosmic turn. By nature, the scholastics meant human nature. Thus, grace meant a gift to that nature which elevated it beyond its own resources. In stressing the contrast between mere human nature and its gracing as supernatural, the scholastics did not consider connecting the supernatural to the rest of the universe. Given what we know now, that human nature evolved out of cosmic nature, then the question of grace and the supernatural must also take into account the nature of the cosmos out of which the human evolved. These considerations suggest that the scholastic notion of the supernatural needs to be expanded.

This means that an expanded understanding of the supernatural takes into account human formation not only in the sphere of the cultural but also of the natural. The gifting of human nature is also the gifting of the givenness of human nature. The givenness of human nature includes the brain as well as the entire body, the material culture as well as the spiritual culture, the technology as well as the arts, all that makes us human. In a theological cosmology, the supernatural is the gifting of the givenness that makes us human, the gifting not merely giving life to the given but creating a place of life abundant.

A Theological Definition of Beauty

The role of grace in natural beauty suggests a revision of the definition of beauty. Although the classical definition of beauty, unity-in-variety, is still helpful, it does not grasp beauty's spiritual dimension. Let me suggest, then, a theological definition of beauty. *Beauty is the sign of life abundant known only by being enjoyed.* To see beauty as a sign allows a crucial distinction between beauty and the beautiful, the experience of beauty. Without the distinction one would not be able to claim that there is beauty in what the world considers ugly. This is important to the theologian who would assert that beauty can be seen in the agonized face of the crucified Christ. Similarly, it allows the theologian to say that not all that the world considers beautiful is an experience of true beauty.

In other words, beauty as a sign preserves its divine origins but allows for human experience. Beauty is a sign that straddles heaven and earth. Beauty as sign also means a meaningful aesthetics is possible. Beauty, like all signs, must be interpreted.

Aesthetics is the science that guides human interpretation of beauty. This is the true meaning of the beautiful.

Let me also suggest that this understanding of beauty may also be a way to expand our understanding of what the church knows as sacramentals. Sacramentals in Roman Catholic theology have usually been the poor sisters of sacraments. The canonical view of sacramentals sees them as "sacred signs by which spiritual effects are signified and are obtained by the intercession of the Church."[31] If we interpret this definition by beginning with sacraments, then sacramentals appear to be mere signs of sacraments. With Vatican II, however, came a hint that sacramentals may be more than mere derivatives of sacraments. *Sacrosanctum Concilium*, for example, considered what makes a sacramental. It concludes, "there is hardly any proper use of material things which cannot thus be directed toward the sanctification of men and the praise of God."[32]

Such an expansive view of sacramentals opens up the possibility of seeing in them a cosmic dimension. The entire cosmos is sprinkled with signs that have the power to sanctify the human. This makes perfect sense if the human, as Teilhard saw, is indeed the aim of the universe. But which are those cosmic signs that are sacramentals? They are the endless forms in the universe whose beauty is enjoyed as abundant life in the human creature. As such, human evolution was the inescapable end of a cosmos, a universe awash in striking beauty. For beauty is meant to be enjoyed. This also means that human evolution, evolved to enjoy the beauty of the cosmos, is also a manifestation of a cosmic collaboration of sanctification with Christ and the Holy Spirit. This insight implies, importantly, that there is a cosmic dimension to the church and that sanctification is the true work of evolution.

The cosmic dimension of the church means that its mission goes beyond those baptized into the church. The body of Christ breathes the Holy Spirit not only "in" for the faithful but also "out" for the cosmos. The church is holy, catholic, apostolic, and, let me suggest, cosmic. The church is headed not simply toward the city of God but to the garden of God. This means there is a dimension to the church that has been neglected but ought no longer be ignored. I believe how the church sees its mission vis-à-vis the cosmos will determine its life in the twenty-first century. This cosmic mission, again, is not one of mere survival in an increasingly toxic environment but the sanctification of the cosmos, the gift of life abundant to the environment.

Thus, the church in its cosmic dimension reveals the true work of evolution, that is, sanctification. For this reason evolution is a work *in* progress but not necessarily *of* progress. Sanctification is more than progress. Sanctification has more to do with reconciliation and communion than with simply advancing to a higher level. If sanctification were simply an individual reaching a higher level, then it would be a solely private affair. If sanctification were simply the advancement of a society to a more advanced form of functionality, then sanctification would be a mere instrumentality. No, sanctification, in cosmic terms, means the coming together of heaven and earth but this is not the same as advancing to a new level of achievement. Rather, sanctification is a work of remarkable beauty. It is a beauty that comes out of a work that knows of struggle and suffering but also peace and joy. In other words, it is a work of human formation. Thus, evolution in a theological cosmology is essentially fulfilled in human sanctification. This means as well that it is a work that sacramentalizes the world. And this, in turn, means that such work is the cosmic mission of the church.

Enjoying and En-Joying

This cosmic mission of the church involves enjoying the life abundant known in the beauty that is the gift of the Holy Spirit to the givenness of the living forms of the cosmos. By enjoying, however, I mean more than mere pleasure. Enjoying has two profound dimensions, enjoying and en-joying. The sacramental enjoyment of human sanctification has both a receptive and active part. Human sanctification, in its most profound meaning, is the receiving or enjoying of beauty and the creating or en-joyment of beauty in beautiful forms. To en-joy means to charge that which is enjoyed with a joy imagined from our imagination as well as receiving the fruits of such imagining. Indeed, the *donum* and *datum* of the cosmos is replicated in the *donum* and *datum* of human sanctification. In other words, human sanctification involves both gift and giving, creating and appreciating, en-joying and enjoying.

Nowhere do we find this manifested most strongly than in the liturgical and devotional art of the church. Art historians continue to puzzle how a tradition that has as a divine commandment the forbidding of graven images could have erupted into a history of strikingly beautiful musical, visual, architectural, and performative forms.[33] Like the endless forms most beautiful of the cosmos, the church produces an endless variety of beautiful forms. Even more interesting, the history of dogma concerning the arts in the church reveals this succession of beautiful forms in the church comes out of struggle and in fits and starts just as the history of evolution of living forms does in the cosmos. This ties the ends of the cosmos to the ends of the church through the endless forms most beautiful created in their respective histories.

That church and cosmos mirror each other in the creation of beautiful forms means there is another aspect to the endless forms most beautiful of both. Beauty enjoyed and en-joyed, at its most profound, is also the taste and the partial realization of a cosmos about to be transformed. In other words, Beauty has an eschatological dimension. It is a dimension enjoyed in its dynamism and made dynamic in its en-joyment. We taste the world-to-come in the en-joying of the world-that-is. We become part of the world-to-come by imagining it into being. As such, this is not an eschatology seen as the future breaking proleptically into the present. It is about imagining and enjoying into being a place of life abundant marked by striking beauty.

More profoundly it means collaborating with Christ and the Spirit in the evolutionary sanctification of the cosmos. It means creating a place of life abundant in the cosmos of striking beauty. It is, furthermore, what marks us as truly human and why we are unique as a creature in the universe. Nowhere is this clearer than in the field of paleoanthropology. It is here where cosmic sanctification is revealed as we discover the struggle of our first ancestors, the first humans, a struggle not merely to survive but to find a place of life abundant. In their struggle, they left parts of their world, their imaginings of a world of striking beauty. They left us bits and pieces of the garden of God, signs of the possibility of an abundant life. Indeed they left us Beauty yet to be en-joyed.

5

The Garden of God

Toward a Theological Cosmology

So what has been concluded toward a theological cosmology? First, let us return to the original inspiration for such a cosmology: Teilhard's vision of the cosmic Christ at the heart of matter bringing all things to be one in, with, and through him. As such, Teilhard's vision is a mix of science, philosophy, and theology that also serves as a profound spirituality. As such, it is a spiritual theology that I believe is desperately needed for the twenty-first century. I distill this spiritual theology to a simple question: Are we at home in the cosmos? Answering that question has taken us to consider many theological questions that are profoundly interconnected defining the contours of a theological cosmology.

We noted, for example, that a theological cosmology has as much to do with place as with the future. The various meanings of place enables traditional theological language to address the strong sense of dynamism in creation that the natural sciences have revealed. Place can do so because it cannot be simply described in terms of an exterior. Place includes an interior dimension. Bachelard helped us see such a dimension. He described in terms of an imagination of intimate inmensity actual in space and time. For this reason, place not only marks a location in the cosmos, it also allows us to call the cosmos home.

The interiority of place also allows us to ask about the "what-ness" of things—"What is this place?" is a meaningful question. Even more important, the interior aspect of place also allows us to ask a related but different question: "Where is this place?" In a purely physical cosmology this is not a meaningful question. Particles exist in a void. Material particles are nowhere. They simply are. Indeed, material particles go nowhere. They simply go. In a cosmology of place, however, "Where is this place?" is a meaningful question. This is crucial in a theological cosmology.

If we cannot ask the *where* of place, we also cannot ask where things are going. And if we cannot ask where things are going then there is no intelligible way to speak of the future. Indeed, this is why place is crucial to our understanding of the future. Future understood without reference to place remains a temporal abstraction. Place gives the future intimacy. As such, it allows the future to enter our poetic imagination and find a meaningul reference there. In other words, place allows the future to be imagined. This is crucial to Christian hope. If we cannot meaningfully refer to the future, if we cannot give it a place, if it can not find reference in the human poetic imagination, then Christian hope of a new creation cannot be entertained intelligibly. Introducing the category of place gives rise to a cosmic view of nature where all things have a name (their "what-ness") and a destination (their "where-ness"). Evolution in a cosmology of place now takes on a more profound meaning.

Rethinking evolution in terms of place allows us to see how it involves the "what-ness" and "where-ness" of the cosmos. This means that space and time may not be adequate categories to understand our natural world. Space and time encourage a view of the world as material particles interacting in an empty void. In such a view, only efficient causality makes sense. Such a view, however, is drastically reductionist. Fortunately, new studies of complex, dynamic systems allow an ancient category to be brought into cosmology to correct such a reductionist view—form. Classically, form asks about the "what-ness" of things. As such, it addresses one of the main questions asked in a cosmology of place. Unfortunately, classical form does not ask about the "where-ness" of things. This question is important, however, in a dynamic universe. Fortunately new studies in the natural sciences suggest there is an alternative to the classical understanding of form—dynamic living form.

Nonequilibrium thermodynamics, for example, gave us a first clue to the kind of form that allows us to ask the "where-ness" of things. Living things, in particular, are defined by a boundary allowing energy to come into the interior and energy to go out to the exterior. In other words, the "where-ness" of living things is found in open systems defined by a boundary. More importantly, open, dynamic systems are marked by forms of striking, dynamic beauty. These forms emerge from the "where-ness" of open, dynamic systems simultaneously revealing the "what-ness" of the system. Now an expanded understanding of form becomes possible. Classical form knew little of directed dynamic process such as those that exist in open systems. Open, dynamic systems, however, allow us to make the leap from classical form to dynamic, living forms. If classical form allowed us to ask about the "what-ness" of things, then dynamic, living form allows us to ask about their "where-ness." Indeed, in these systems, beautiful dynamic forms are symptoms of the "what-ness" and the "where-ness" of all systems that exchange energy in the universe.

With our new understanding of form we can now ask two valuable questions made problematic in a physical cosmology. We can ask, for example, What is a dragonfly? and Where do they live? Please note that an answer to these questions will take us immediately into the interconnectedness of the dragonfly with its predators and its prey, with the habitat in which it lives, and all sorts of other factors that a purely physical cosmology cannot entertain. More important, a cosmology that allows us to ask the "what" and the "where" of things opens up the interior dimension of all creatures, a dimension characterized by beautiful forms.

This dimension accounts for the sensed truthfulness that poetic reference to the beauty of natural forms express. For example, the great Jesuit poet, Gerard Manley Hopkins, tells us in a famous poem that "as kingfishers catch fire, dragonflies draw flame."[1] Does not Hopkins here grasp a natural truth about kingfishers and dragonflies? Virginia Stem Owens grasps the nature of such truth:

> There are no phenomena without perception, no perception without attention, no attention without desire. Beauty is in the eye of the beholder, says the cynic. Precisely. But he says more than he knows. More elusive than engrams is a code in our consciousness that recognizes beauty when it sees it, that builds it out of molecular movement. But an even more elemental code desires, searches for, insists upon beauty.[2]

Let me suggest that this mysterious but profound truth is sensed through the intimacy of place that beautiful forms abide. For example, kingfishers and dragonflies not only live in their native habitat; they are made beautiful because of it. This connection between life and beauty can only be found in the depth of a cosmic interior dimension. The intimate interior dimension that kingfishers and dragonflies enjoy is present to our poetic imagination precisely because we are creatures sublimely attuned to all that is intimate and interior. We are grasped by the intimacy of place that kingfishers and dragonflies enjoy so that we, too, may en-joy it with them. In such en-joyment, beauty points for us where the intimacy of home may be found. It is for this reason that the "what" and "where" of kingfishers and dragonflies are important questions for us. The intimacy suggested by questions of "what" and "where" are crucial to the sense of place. In summary, open systems exhibit not only a "what" but also a "where" suggesting a new category of form—form-in-flux or dynamic, living form. Dynamic forms reveal the theological cosmos to be a place of beauty, a place of endless living forms most beautiful. Indeed, such forms reveal the very intimacy of the human habitat. It is a place of life, and, even more than this, a place *for* abundant life.

From a broader view, living, dynamic forms reveal a mix of "what-ness" and "where-ness" to the cosmos. They suggest a cosmos bounded by an interior and an exterior geography. Indeed, our cosmos itself may be seen as an open system. There is a boundary that brings life to the cosmos and breathes fire into its equations, a boundary where the limitations of the material meets the openness of the spiritual, the place of interchange that defines the what-ness and where-ness of the cosmos itself. I am referring to the boundary defining heaven and earth. Along this boundary, among the many living forms that have evolved, a new form of life is evolving. This new form of life belongs to the species known as *Homo sapiens*. It is the most elusive of forms to grasp for it is also the most spiritual.

In such a cosmology, a cosmos in which a new form of life is evolving out of the intersection of heaven and earth, the theologian must address anew the Church's understanding of Christ, the one who revealed the intersection of heaven and earth. This means addressing the ancient tradition on the cosmic dimension of Christ. A new look at the cosmic Christ requires a deeper understanding of the work of the Holy Spirit. The cosmic Christ of the Church Fathers must now include the cosmic dimension of the Spirit who hovered over the waters at the beginning and now renews the face of the earth. A cosmic Christology, in other words, requires an equally cosmic pneumatology. If Christ is the Form of salvation, the Spirit crafts Christ's Form onto each of us and onto the cosmos with a myriad of living, beautiful forms. If Christ has been seen as the *Logos* that brings reason and order to the universe, it is the Spirit that breathes fire and life and beauty into that order.

This combination of divine reason and divine fire, of exquisite order and entangled life, of endless forms-in-flux most beautiful, leads us to a new appreciation of what is meant by beauty. Beauty is more than something to behold in forms but also a power that forms. Beauty seen in cosmic breadth rather than museum walls reveals a dimension of itself that the modern world ignored and the postmodern world could not see. Beauty is a sign of abundant life known only by being enjoyed.

Thus, beauty, in its cosmic sense, refers to a new form of life, abundant life. Abundant life can only be found at one place—the intersection of heaven and earth. Abundant life is spirituality for a theological cosmology. It emphasizes the physicality of the spiritual rather than opposes it. As such, it becomes the prime category for our final reflection. This means we must now turn to the nature of the place where heaven and earth intersect. It is here that we will find the creature that defines abundant life: *Homo sapiens*. If the human is distinct from all other creatures, it is because we have one foot on heaven and the other on earth. Indeed, we embody that cosmic boundary. Thus, we must turn to where heaven and earth intersect. There we shall find the human phenomenon, a phenomenon inextricable from beauty, and our true home in the cosmos.

Where Heaven and Earth Intersect

Where do heaven and earth intersect? The traditional answer in theology has been the human creature. But what boundary does the human creature straddle? What sort of place is it that a boundary defines not by circumscription but by splitting asunder? The tradition tells us it is a garden. It is at the boundary of the garden of Eden, at the moment of expulsion, that we recognized ourselves as human. There we sensed ourselves to be a troubled creature, tragic in a dignity we ourselves marred. The essential reference to the fall of the human is the garden. For this reason, it ought to alert the theologian that to try to understand the fall of the human without a cosmic reference may lead to unpalatable conclusions.

Perhaps this is why the Church clings to its doctrine of the fall of the angels. It points to a profound cosmic dimension to evil and human suffering. It is actually necessary if one is to make sense of the serpent in the garden of Eden. In other words, the fall of the angels and the fall of the human are doctrines mysteriously intertwined. One cannot make sense of the one without the other. The key, I believe, to their mysterious entanglement is to be found by locating the doctrine known as original sin in a theological cosmology. For this reason, we must turn to a text that has striking similarities to Genesis 2, the account of the fall of the human. In this text a fallen angel, Satan, also attempts to tempt the human and make him fail. As in Genesis 2, this is done to show the Creator the lack of integrity of God's human creation. In other words, I am speaking of the book of Job.

It is puzzling that so much of our doctrine of creation has focused on Genesis rather the book of Job. After all, in Job we have the Creator speaking directly about God's creation. The book of Job carries many meanings. I wish only to point out one meaning that has been overlooked in our day. The book of Job is not only about justifying a belief in an all-powerful and benevolent God; it is also about justifying the human creature. Satan wagers God that Job, representing all humanity, fails as God's human creature. In other words, Job as human is the glory of the Lord. Satan wagers otherwise. If Job fails to measure up to God's expectations, then it also means that God fails. God's glory will be seen as an illusion when it comes to the human creature.

This means the book of Job is not simply about the justification of God in the light of evil, that is, a theodicy. The book of Job perhaps has more to do with the justification of the human caught in the web of evil, in other words, an anthropodicy. What makes human justification in the book of Job interesting is that it revolves around a bet. Satan bets God the human creature is not what God intended him and her to be. It is not immediately clear, however, how the bet will be settled. What will satisfy Satan that he has lost the wager? Gustavo Gutiérrez in his book, *On Job*, gives what I consider a profound answer: "It is important that we be clear from the outset that the theme of the Book of Job is not precisely suffering . . . but rather how to speak of God in the midst of suffering."[3] Indeed, God admonishes Job's friends: "for you have not spoken of me what is right, as my servant Job has done" (Job 42:8).

What justifies Job's humanity is that in spite of his suffering he was able to speak well of God. As Job's dialogue indicates this does not mean excusing God of accountability but reminding God of God's integrity. God's integrity, however, is to be found in the whole creation, as the whirlwind makes clear—"Where were you when I laid down the foundations of the earth?" (Job 38:4). Seen this way, perhaps there is a new way to look at the whirlwind's address to Job. Job speaks well of God when he insisted in God's integrity. But what about Job's integrity? What makes Job truly human? Perhaps the whirlwind's address is less a scolding than it is an invitation. Job's human integrity lies in being able to enter into the very wisdom of God's plans for God's creation.

But here is the catch. God's creation has its own integrity. It is not a machine with which one can tinker with abandon. Job is not being invited to reverse-engineer God's creation so that he can create beautiful creatures like God. The wisdom being offered Job is not one of engineering design or wanton consuming but one fitted perfectly to the human creature: to help bring abundance of life and beauty to what is already a marvelous creation. Bringing abundance to the natural has more to do with gardening than engineering. Yet it is in this sort of work where the whirlwind hints of Job's true justification.

The few sentences describing how God restores Job's lands and families could be interpreted not as direct divine intervention but Job's newfound wisdom that allows him to bring abundance out of the natural and social world around him. This interpretation makes more sense since it speaks directly to Satan's wager. Because of God's integrity, the human has integrity. The human creature will not destroy God's creation but will make it even more marvelous.

If we take God's integrity as the starting point in any reflection on evil, then justifying the human creation becomes our interpretative key to doctrines that refer to evil. One such doctrine is that of original sin. It is as much a story about God's integrity as it is about human failing. As a story of God's integrity, it means that Genesis 2 has a profound connection to the book of Job. The story of the expulsion from the garden is also the story of the justification of the human creature. This means that the expulsion from the garden includes an invitation to enter into the very heart of creation. By having to build a garden instead of merely taking care of one, the human must learn first-hand the very heart of creation's integral processes.

Here is where evolutionary theories about the human creature can help bring a cosmic dimension to Christian understanding of human falleness. Paleoanthropology has been asking questions about human evolution that theology ought to engage. What is surprising is that these questions revolve around beauty.

Beauty, Ever Ancient, Ever New

On September 8, 1940, seventeen-year-old Marcel Ravidat and three of his friends were looking for a lost treasure in the woods near in the woods near Montignac, France. The villagers had talked for years of a secret underground tunnel and Marcel thought he could find it. No one really knows what happened that day. One account tells that Robot, Marcel's dog, became stuck in a hole. As the boys tried to pull Robot out of the hole, they discovered what appeared to be a bottomless hole. The boys went into the hole but without a light they did not get very far. The boys returned five days later with a lantern. They had not gone in very far when what appeared to be a hole turned into a huge cavern. As they looked up, they saw on the ceiling red cows full of life and vitality, paintings that had not seen the light of day for about thirty thousand years. The boys had discovered the cave of Lascaux, a place of beauty and one of the sites where evidence of our earliest humanity can be found.

Lascaux is not unique, however. Other caves with such ancient paintings have since been found. What surprises many is how much they are moved by their beauty. Jean Clottes, one of France's distinguished experts on prehistory, was one of these. "I remember standing in front of the paintings of the horses facing the rhinos and being profoundly moved by the artistry. Tears were running down my cheeks. I was witnessing one of the world's great masterpieces."[4] Clottes's response ought to make us pause for two reasons. First, it should make us wonder that the first humans were capable of such strikingly beautiful works. Second, and more marvelously, it should make us wonder that, millennia later, we are still able of being moved by their beauty.

It is striking, then, that few theologians have turned to the recent discussions in paleoanthropology. It would seem that in these discussions a theologian might find great insights into the meaning of the doctrine of the *imago Dei*. More importantly, paleoanthropology offers new insights into the nature of human suffering. It seems inexcusable for a contemporary discussion of evil or of human suffering to avoid the findings concerning human evolution.

Perhaps one of the most interesting findings is one that affirms a conviction of Christian theology. The human creature is, in a special sense, unique from all other creatures. For example, the noted paleoanthropologist Ian Tattersall, in his book *Becoming Human: Evolution and Human Uniqueness*, argues, "We human beings are indeed mysterious animals. We are linked to the living world, but we are sharply distinguished by our cognitive powers, and much of our behavior is conditioned by abstract and symbolic concerns."[5] By abstract and symbolic concerns, Tattersall means the wondrous evidence of art, music, and symbols found in places where the first humans gathered, such as in the Lascaux cave. In other words, humans are unique as creatures. What distinguishes us is the capacity of our imagination and the creativity to create works of art, music, and symbol that reflect that imagination.

Ian Tattersall's conclusions that tie human distinctiveness with the marvelous evidence of art, music, and symbols in paleolithic sites reflect the growing consensus among paleoanthropologists that prehistoric art marks a crucial development in human evolution.[6] These discoveries are of direct relevance to the theologian not merely because they illuminate the origins of the human creature but because they reveal something crucial about what it means to be human. For most paleoanthropologists, this has something to do with the nature of the human mind. The mind is what makes the human creature unique among all creatures.

This approach is understandable but perhaps reductionistic, at least if by mind one means the mere capacity to know. Is cognition the sole defining trait of the human creature? If so, then yes, perhaps most paleoanthropologists are right. The human mind is what makes us unique among creatures. Yet what Tattersall points to as human distinctiveness is the human imagination and our ability to make a cultural world out of that imagination. And not merely a world simply to live in, but a world of beauty, music, and art. Indeed, identifying mental capacity as the unique category of human creatureliness tends to dismiss the aesthetic sense in prehistoric art.[7] Such art is seen more as the product of a mind making rational decisions as opposed to an imagination creating beautiful forms.

J. Wentzel van Huyssteen, for example, warns against "classifying prehistoric imagery exclusively as art, or as the origins or beginnings of art."[8] Nonetheless, he finds such paleolithic imagery certainly evokes beauty even if they were not originally supposed to be "aesthetic" objects. David Lewis-Williams, in his book *The Mind in the Cave*, is less ambiguous about paleolithic art and the aesthetic sense of beauty:

> an aesthetic sense (if there is such a thing) was developed after the first appearance of art in the sense of image-making; it was a consequence, not a cause, of art-making, a consequence, moreover, that real people living in specific times, places, and social circumstances constructed, not one they inherited in the make-up of their brains.[9]

Both these distinguished authors either disengage the beautiful from art or find their relationship problematic. This should not surprise the theologian, however. The disengagement of the beautiful from art belongs to a three-hundred-year-old secularizing tradition begun in the Enlightenment.

The distinguished professor of aesthetics Nicholas Wolsterstorff coined this tradition the "Grand Modern Narrative of Art." The Grand Modern Narrative of the Arts is the view that art developed progressively until it found its liberation in the eighteenth century as an object of disinterested perceptual contemplation.[10] Such a tradition creates what John Dewey in *Art and Experience* calls "museum art."[11] In other words, art, that is, modern art, is something to be "looked at." But the kind of art to which van Huyssteen and Lewis-Williams are referring is not that kind of art. Paleolithic art is not "museum art." Such art was part of daily life. It was art to be "lived with," not "looked at."

No wonder van Huyssteen and Lewis-Williams find it difficult to attach the aesthetic sense of beauty to a work of art. There is no category in modern aesthetics for art that is "lived with"! Modern aesthetics through the Grand Modern Narrative of the Arts has reduced the number of senses that those who enjoy these marvelous works engage. Disinterested perceptual contemplation corresponds more to a clinical engagement of mental reasoning than the experience of a life-giving imagination. The experience of a life-giving imagination, however, has, as John Dewey so clearly saw, more to do with religious experience than with the exercise of the intellect.

It is for this reason that modern aesthetics rules out as "art" most devotional and liturgical works.[12] By not being aware about the religious aesthetic sense that corresponds to devotional and liturgical art, paleoanthropologists may be missing out on a potentially powerful interpreting tool. Devotional art, for example, does not follow the Grand Modern Narrative of the Arts. It is more for "living with" than "looking at." More important, devotional art involves sharing the hopes, struggles, and sufferings of those it touches. Indeed, devotional art expresses a tragic consciousness. It is art that engages a consciousness of a need of salvation and aims to be a guide in finding a way toward that salvation. If paleolithic art is, as I suspect, devotional, or even a kind of liturgical art, then there is a dimension to human uniqueness that has yet to be explored in paleoanthropology. The human creature represents a new form of life.

By a new form of life I mean that life to which Jesus refers when he tells Satan: "Man does not live by bread alone." It is foolish to believe one can easily define such life. It is fundamentally elusive. Yet we have names for it. People have called it spirituality, religiosity, piety, and many other names. All of these are useful in that they denote one or another facet of a many-faceted living reality. Nonetheless, none of these do justice to the new form of life into which the human was born. Perhaps the closest I can come to denoting its most salient characteristic is that it is a life lived abundantly. It is life expansive of the limits that our frailty imposes upon us. It is life expansive even of the limits the self imposes yet paradoxically expands the self. It is life meant to be lived not merely physically but abundantly. It is abundant life.

I can only think of one form of life that is a good analogy to life abundant—the garden. The essence of a garden is what Gabriel Marcel once referred to as "creative receptivity." By this he meant renouncing "the claim that . . . we have the power to make [things] dependent only on ourselves."[13] For what is most truly enjoyed in a garden is the sense of gift. The experience of gift is an essential component of an abundant life. It is also the heart of religious experience.

I do not know if the first humans dreamt of gardens, but if they did it is because gardens must have been our parents' first religious experience. If so, then it is easier to see the beauty of the images in the Lascaux cave as images of a garden, or, rather, images of a devotion to a garden. Yet to dream of gardens reveals a kind of judgment about life as experienced daily. Devotion to the garden has an eschatological zing. It is not simply devotion of what could be but a critique of what has been. Gardens are both an ultimate commentary about what human achievement could be and a reproach against anything regarded as ultimate human achievement. We enter gardens to get a taste of what life lived abundantly might be.

As such, gardens are peculiar works of art. They are works of the imagination that one can actually enter. Yet, of all works, gardens reveal most about the nature of the universe and the human phenomenon within. For this reason, we now turn to the garden to see if we can find the true human phenomenon, the new form of life, life abundant existing where heaven intersects earth.

A Garden Trail

Perhaps no art is more a "living with" than the works of art that are gardens. Gardens are meant to be enjoyed by being "lived with." For this reason, gardens may have been the first form of devotional art. But did the first humans, our ancestors, ever dream of gardens? Indeed, did they ever dream of paradise, a garden of Eden? There is good reason to believe so. Tattersall puts it this way:

> Human beings are the result of the same evolutionary process that produced the entire vast diversity of living things. Yet we cannot help but think of ourselves as somehow significantly "different" from the rest of nature. There's plenty of justification for this. . . . As far as we know, for example, we're alone in nature in being able to contemplate our place in it.[14]

David Cooper, in his book *A Philosophy of Gardens*, feels that this ability to contemplate our place in nature is the essence of gardens.[15] If this is the case, then the first humans, our parents, must have, like us, also contemplated their place in nature by envisioning gardens.

Yet the role of gardens in human thought and sensibility has fallen in hard times. I believe much of the reason has to do with the great disconnect that modern and postmodern society has made between beauty, art, and life. The Grand Modern

Narrative of Art now present in contemporary society has served to make art something to be looked at, not something to be lived with. It has commodified art. Between the auction blocks of Sotheby's and the marketing strategies of art galleries we have lost our belief in a sensibility to beauty. It is interesting, then, that "what contemporary art galleries rarely offer people—beauty, delicacy, or grandeur, for example—gardens are still allowed to do."[16]

More important, such beauty, delicacy, and grandeur are, in gardens, the symptoms of what philosophy once knew as "the good life." Gardens fuse art and nature as a way of envisioning or embodying what the "good life" is. In this one can see why gardens matter and matter deeply. A successful fusing of art and nature depends on profound insight into the relationship between human creative activity and the world. Yet it is this relationship that contains the mystery of what it means to be human. As Cooper puts it, "the garden is an 'epiphany' of the relationship between human creative activity, the world, and the 'ground' of the world."[17] Perhaps the greater mystery is how attention to this relationship has been ignored in contemporary theology. For in this relationship lies the vital impulse behind religious experience.

The Tragic Choice

This vital impulse is the flip side of the "good life." By this I mean the tragic sense of life. We know that our lives are not what they should be. This knowledge is mysterious in itself. We have no experience of a perfect life. We have no experience of the life we should have had by which to contrast the life we have. Yet the contrast exists in every human experience. We know suffering even though we cannot find any rational grounds for such knowledge. In other words, we don't really know how we know we suffer. Yet there would be no gardens if there were no suffering.

The garden, after all, implicitly questions the status quo of everyday living. Paradoxically, gardens not only value life as we know it but also embody life as we think it should be. Robin Matthews refers to this paradox as a "sinuous ambiguity":

> On the one hand, the drive toward an ultimate ground of meaning presses on ancient memories of a paradise graced by natural repose and ripened creaturehood. These memories, on the other hand, have been darkened by the withering harvest of hardship that has separated matured humanity from paradise. But these paradisial images arise from the depths of the fallen present rather than some prelapsarian past. The discontinuity between paradisial and present worlds presses home a vital religious quandary. How can humanity feel the loss of a paradisial creaturehood that it never possessed in the first place?[18]

Whether or not theology can agree with Matthews about the absence of a prelapsarian past, this paradox, the tension between the immediacy and inaccessibility, of another time and place where no tear was ever shed, emerges from *this* time and place. Its roots are to be found in the "ground" of this world.

Thus, gardens query the relationship between life in this world and the "ground" of this world. Gardens are the premier locus of a theological cosmology. As such, they reveal a cosmic element in human suffering. The roots of our tragic sense of life must somehow be buried in the evolutionary process that brought forth our first parents. A simple observation may help make this point. Whatever can be said about *Homo sapiens*, one aspect can be pointed out: physically, we must be the least adapted of all creatures. We are born without fur to keep us warm. We are born without strength to overcome our prey. We are born without any physical advantage in terms of hearing, sight, smell, taste, or touch. In other words, physically the human species appears to be a monumental evolutionary failure.

The emergence of the human in evolution is marked not by our physical fitness to the environment but our frailty. Whatever evolutionary theory one might hold, human physical frailty must be the primary *datum* that such a theory must explain. No other animal is so physically minimally adapted to its environment. Perhaps here the roots of our sense of a lost garden of Eden can be found. Physical frailty was, after all, the immediate consequence of the expulsion from Eden. Can we imagine an evolutionary tale of Eden? Could there have been a kind of evolutionary catastrophe in our distant evolutionary past? Could it have been that the beginnings of a human-like creativity in not-fully-human species led to some sort of evolutionary crisis? Could there have been a cosmic choice between a powerful spiritual creativity or a superior physically adapted body in the evolutionary process that led to the first humans? Could a choice for spiritual creativity have led to the emergence of a species frail in body but creative in spirit?

Perhaps not, and it may be foolish to try to propose such a possibility. Nonetheless, if the doctrine of the fall is to be something more than an irrelevant myth, if it is to gain a cosmic dimension, the attempt must be made. I would begin with Teilhard's special view of evolution.[19] If species, as Teilhard thought, can come to be by some sort of will to exploit an adaptive opportunity, then perhaps somewhere in the evolutionary process the rise of a new kind of creature creativity led to a kind of cosmic choice. The human-to-be may well have been on his and her way to a superior physical adaptation but then found the lure of new creative powers more advantageous than physical superiority. The human-to-be then made a tragic choice. The nascent human made a choice in favor of spiritual creativity over and against superior physicality.

This is a tragic choice insofar that creativity is difficult to control. Creativity has unintended consequences that are hard to predict. More often than not, it destabilizes what it touches. If spiritual creativity is the key to our place in the cosmos, it is also one of the most potent destabilizing forces in the cosmos.[20] Here perhaps lies our tragic sense of our humanity. Our creativity far surpasses our ability to control its consequences. That which gives an awesome dignity to the human is also that which takes us into unexpected tragic consequences.

If the above is true, then the sense of a lost garden of Eden then has a basis in human experience. We carry its memory in the physical frailty of our human flesh and a spiritual creativity we scarcely know how to control. Nonetheless, in this tragic choice also is found a shining hope. The human species has yet to live up to its full potential. What is human has not yet come fully to be. This, I believe, will take place when humanity learns to control its potent yet dangerous spiritual creativity.[21]

In Search of Eden

Perhaps here lies the deeper significance of paleolithic art, perhaps of all art. While the essence of art is elusive if not downright impossible to define, there are two aspects of art that should not go unnoticed. One aspect concerns how art addresses physical frailty. Art aims to give an experience of a world that is just beyond our grasp. Whether it is abstract expressionism or *trompe l'oeil*, Gregorian chant or atonal music, the spirit of art is to take us to the boundary of our physical senses to explore the interiority of the world around us. As such, art is deeply spiritual precisely because it has its roots in our physical frailty.

The other aspect is more subtle. Art is also an unsurpassed human achievement. It is not simply a matter of talent. Somehow a dangerous and unwieldy creativity finds enough control as to bear creations of remarkable beauty. This is a remarkable achievement, for human creativity often serves to bring indescribable suffering. Paradoxically, human creativity can serve to enhance our humanity or diminish it. Indeed, those gifted with such creativity often find that it can destroy them. In any case, controlled creativity is one of the great achievements of a work of art. What art, and paleolithic art in particular, can teach us is that the key to reaching our full human potential is a controlled creativity issuing forth a life-giving beauty, an abundant spiritual environment of beauty.

Perhaps this is why gardens play such an important role in our cosmic mythologies. Gardens are, if anything, works of remarkably controlled spiritual creativity of great beauty. Carolyn Merchant, in *Reinventing Eden*, tells us that the search for a garden of Eden is "perhaps the most important mythology humans have developed to make sense of their relationship to the Earth."[22] The garden of Eden represents an expansive creativity as home to a frail humanity. It was an environment of stunning beauty. As such, it also represents the offer of an abundant life. No wonder the search for such a garden has been such a universal human trait. It is the heart of the spiritual quest.

Gardens, however, exist in various forms. They are not always filled with rose bushes and flowers. More important, gardens are expressions of a deep spiritual quest, a quest for our very humanity. Merchant insightfully describes how this quest manifests itself in the West today.

Where is this Eden? It is not in the Mesopotamian lands of the pre-Christian era. It is the new downtown square on the promenade in Anytown, California. The square is replete with fountains, grassy knolls, meandering streams, and benches for passersby. Along each side of the river flowing through the square are the shops of the revived cityscape. Gracefully arched bridges connect the two sides of the street, and the shops face the greenbelt along the river. The stores are those found in hundreds of towns across the nation: Borders books, Starbucks Coffee, Cost Plus, World Market, Noah's Bagels, Banana Republic, and Jamba Juice. This is the new American Eden.[23]

This downtown square may not be a garden in the common sense. It is not even a modern Lascaux cave but Merchant's description of the "American Eden" describes a place filled with the same longing found in the paleolithic art of our first ancestors.

The problem with the "American Eden" is that it fails as a garden. It is an environment of life consumed, not an environment of life abundant. The "American Eden" commodifies creativity in a vain attempt to avoid creativity's main reference, our physical frailty. Tragically, commodifying spiritual creativity leads to spiritual creativity being consumed and our physical frailty becoming even more frail. In the "American Eden" the serpent offering what it cannot give is an economy that commodifies spiritual creativity.

Nonetheless, the "American Eden" does help us understand what sort of Eden the ancient spiritual quest is seeking. The opposite of the "American Eden" is a place where spiritual creativity is life-giving gift rather than life-consuming commodity. So how do we return to the true quest? How shall we begin to cultivate a New Eden? By turning to a disciplined creativity aimed at creating a place that seeks not merely to consume life but to live it abundantly. The nature of that discipline has to be a garden discipline. By this I mean a kind of discipline that is part technology and part art, a discipline of creative receptivity to the ground of the world out of which such a place is made. I mean a discipline aimed at producing living forms of remarkable beauty and a beauty that forms our lives. I am speaking of the discipline that exists in the garden of God.

A Disciplined Spiritual Technology

Gardens are made. They do not simply come to be. As such, they are as much technology as they are art. Unfortunately, as mentioned in an earlier chapter, technology in our lifetime has taken on an extremely narrow sense. More insidiously, technology has become the primary means of commodifying spiritual creativity. Indeed, technology today engages the very depths of human imagination and creativity only to package it for the market to be consumed in the "American Eden." But perhaps the most demonic aspect of technology today is its ability to commodify by decontextualizing spiritual creativity.

Spiritual creativity exists in the context of a physical frailty. Technology today removes this vital context of spiritual creativity in order to commodify it.[24] Yet it is physical frailty that entangles in the very heart of the cosmos. Human physical frailty makes us part of the entangled bank of life that so inspired Darwin. It is our foot on the earth that allows us to place our other foot in heaven. A spiritual creativity taken out of its context in physical frailty allows a foothold neither on earth nor in heaven. It is a packaged illusion meant to be consumed while at the same time disengaging us from our vital physical frailty.

Technology does not to be this way. Indeed, the key to the garden of God will be finding a true, human technology. Such technology will be as much art as it is craft. Its aims will be less utilitarian than they will be spiritual. Such technology will continually keep before it its proper mission: to create a life-giving place for human becoming. Such technology will be a disciplined creativity addressing our human frailty. So what sort of discipline would such technology adopt? What sort of principles might such discipline entail?

I do not claim to know the full answer to these questions but I can propose a few elements vital to such a discipline. First, one must understand the twin temptations of a technology that would attempt a garden of Eden. One temptation would be to emphasize the reinventing of Eden; the other the return to Eden.[25] One would take us to a world of technological superiority over the physical world; the other to a world where the physical world rules over human technology. One approach would continually orient us toward the future; the other to the past. I am speaking of a technology, instead, that would neither reinvent Eden nor try to take us back, a technology oriented toward the present. But it would be a present trying to create itself in the light of the past and in anticipation of the future, a present that sees itself as being part of a beginning, a middle, and an end. In other words, the garden of God would be a storied place where past, present, and future come together. This would be one of the first principles of a disciplined spiritual technology.

To be oriented toward the present also means to be oriented toward the gift dimension of the earth. It is a technology aware of human frailty and oriented toward it. It is a technology cautious to disturb the present for it sees its life and its beauty as entangled in a myriad of reciprocal and antagonistic ways. Nonetheless, being oriented toward the present also means a technology aimed at preserving the dynamism of an entangled web of life. As such, it suggests the next principle for a disciplined spiritual technology. A disciplined spiritual technology aims toward the entanglement of beautiful living forms. A technology of entangled life is the heart of a garden technology. It seeks to create a place where life can lead to more life. And to do so beautifully.

Such a discipline partially exists. It is to be found in an aesthetics. As mentioned earlier, the oldest definition of formal beauty is unity-in-variety. As such, this definition serves quite well to describe the formal requirements of any form that one might consider beautiful. Its weakness, however, becomes evident in the ambiguity of the definition. Is beauty, for example, to be found in the unity or the variety of the form? Once you ask that question, a more profound element of beauty becomes evident. It is that element which somehow brings the varied into a unity without losing either the variety or the unity.

Christopher Alexander, in his book *The Phenomenon of Life*, attempts to answer that question by asking the question of what makes a "whole" out of a disparate set of "parts." By looking at living forms he discovered that he could discern in most living forms what he calls "centers." A center refers to the nexus of relationships that form a whole apart from the boundaries that "a whole" implies. For Alexander, the center of an entity exists before the parts. A "part" may exist independently, but becoming a "part" depends upon a relationship between its center and the center of what will become "the whole." Thus, a part can be a whole in itself, and wholes may become parts for other wholes.[26]

In other words, centers are the heart of the entanglement of living forms. What is even more crucial, Alexander found such centers exist in well-designed architectural spaces. True living space actually is life giving by life entangling. Such space has discernable "centers" that bring a diversity of parts into a whole that then becomes a part that can participate in an even larger whole. I find Alexander's discussion of "centers" to be a crucial element in a disciplined spiritual technology. Such a discipline would work with "centers" that entangle human life with all life. It would build a place of life-entangling, life-giving "centers."

"Centers," furthermore, are the key to understanding the aesthetics of beauty as abundant life enjoyed. As the nexus that brings a diverse number of "parts" into a "whole" it not only satisfies the ancient formal requirement of beauty as unity-in-variety; it also helps us extend this requirement to the dynamic beauty of living forms. "Centers," then, are responsible both for the beauty of a single living form but also for the entanglement of such beautiful forms into a greater living form. In other words, "centers" allow us to speak meaningfully of the "what" and "where" of beauty. It is a place, a place of beauty.

Finally, I would also include in such a disciplined spiritual theology the transformation of technology into art. By this I mean transforming our view of technology as creating consumable works of the creative imagination into a view of technology as creating a place of life-giving beauty. Technology as art would be a garden technology, for it would query the role creative activity has in relationship to the world. It would seek the "centers" that are epiphanies of the "ground" of this world. It would discipline its creative genius around these "centers," creating a place not merely to be lived in but to be "lived with."

A place that is "lived-with" and not merely "looked-at" is the true measure of a garden. Gardens, after all, have a natural integrity that human cultural activity must respect. Gardens require a tender reciprocal engagement between the natural and the cultural. In other words, gardens are meant to be "lived-with," not merely "lived-in." Gardens are a place to which one has a relationship. What is the nature of this relationship? What else could it be but devotion? There can be no garden without human devotion. As such, technology would become devotional art. It would be an art of devotion to the earth for the sake of heaven. It would be art that not only is an expression of devotion but also inspires it.

Such a technology would have a profound effect on our overall view of technology today. Technology as devotional art would be technology transformed into gift as opposed to commodity. It would control creativity not by consuming it but by turning it into devotion. As such, technnology would transform our cities into gardens, our interconnected communications into entangled banks of life, our ever-present advertising to liturgies of praise, and our spiritual arrogance that denies our frail relationship to the earth to a life-giving humility acknowledging our frailty before heaven.

The Garden of God

There is more than can be said. Even inspired by and using much of the work of Teilhard de Chardin, this whole proposal is nothing more than a stab at a project of cosmic dimensions. Yet consider the consequences of not beginning such a project. Can theology really not see its true eschatological mission in our day? As we run out of room for an ever-growing population, as the polar caps melt into the sea and the weather becomes more unpredictable and hostile, as we continue to consume ourselves into extinction, can theology not see their eschatological import? These realities, after all, are cosmic realities. They affect us cosmically. Such is the stuff of eschatology. For this reason, a twenty-first-century eschatology will have to be a cosmology.

A twenty-first-century eschatology will also mean looking deeper at the cosmological foundations of the church. In the late twentieth century the church came to see itself as global. The church could no longer ignore the global interconnectedness of economies, religions, cultures, and technologies. Yet global interconnectedness does not begin to address the true interconnectedness that ties all humanity together. That interconnectedness includes heaven and earth. If the church is to be true to its mission, it must recognize that interconnectedness as part of its mission. This means the church must expand its cosmic awareness.

Is it really only a peculiarity of history that a cosmic awareness of the church permeated the Scriptures and theology up to modern times? Is it really only an idiosyncrasy of Paul and the Gospels to discuss explicitly the cosmic dimension of the teachings of the risen Christ? Is it really an accident of culture that the church fathers were preoccupied with the cosmic meaning of church doctrines? If not, then where is the church's cosmic awareness now? Why doesn't it see itself not only as one, holy, catholic, and apostolic, but also as cosmic? I believe that it will. It cannot but turn to cosmology as a way to address the grave crisis we are experiencing today.

In doing so, the Church will find again the cosmic Christ through whom all things were made. The Church will also have to turn to the Spirit who was sent by Christ and the Father, the Lord and Giver of life *and* beauty. It will also have to turn to an eschatology of place rather than of time, for it is not so much a future that is being built by the two "hands" of God. It is a place, and that place is elusive. Tradition has called it a garden. It is more than a pretty metaphor. The garden addresses the relationship of God's most invested creation, the human, with the rest of creation. It is this relation that is most problematic, for it has tragic overtones.

It is, ultimately, the source of human suffering but also of our true human potential. It is a relationship that needs justification not simply to other humans but to the cosmos itself. A theological cosmology turns out to be not only an eschatology but also an anthropodicy.[27] At stake is God's integrity. In the openness of God's own cosmic creativity, a frail creature was allowed to possess an extremely dangerous creativity. That such frailty could bear such creativity, we are told, is the wager that opens up a window into the very identity of God. It also sets up the human mission. We are to find in our frailty, the strength of the Lord.

Ultimately, this means cultivating a garden, the garden of God. It means finding our relationship to the world. It means finding a home in the cosmos. We have some clues to that relationship. The world was created for an entanglement of endless living forms most beautiful. Abundant life found in beauty enjoyed is the sign that marks the road to the garden of God. There is another sign to that road, however. Our humanity is marked by our ability to create works of beauty. These two signs comprise the basis for a garden technology by which to build the garden of God. We are to develop a technology of devotion to place. This place is where earth and heaven intersect. Finding this place and building upon it is the heart of such technology. Moreover, it is a place found not in the past nor in the future but in the present. Here and now, we must begin to build.

We must find the "centers" that create and entangle beautiful, living forms. We must engender devotion to place so we can truly create a place to "live with." We must be guided by human frailty for only human frailty is capable of knowing abundant life. In this, we are to be guided by beauty herself. We will know beauty as a sign known only by being en-joyed, en-joyed into abundant life. We must create a place built by gifts, not commodities. Indeed, we must build a place that is also a gift. In doing so, we will have found our place in the cosmos. We will have built and received the garden of God.

Notes

Preface

1. Charles S. Peirce, "Some Consequences of Four Incapacities," *Journal of Speculative Philosophy*, no. 2 (1868): section 3.

2. I first proposed the notion of an aesthetic insight in *A Wounded Innocence*. Since then I have revised my understanding. For the earlier proposal see Alejandro García-Rivera, *A Wounded Innocence: Sketches for a Theology of Art* (Collegeville, Minn.: Liturgical Press, 2003).

3. Royce makes a distinction between insight and religious insight. For his proposal see Josiah Royce, *The Sources of Religious Insight: Lectures* (New York: Scribner, 1912).

1. At Home in the Cosmos

1. Gary Strieker, "Scientists Agree World Faces Mass Extinction," CNN.com(2002), http://archives.cnn.com/2002/TECH/science/08/23/green.century.mass.extinction/index.html.

2. As they put it, "The current extinction event is due to human activity, paving the planet, creating pollution, many of the things that we are doing today. . . . The Earth might well lose half of its species in our lifetime." Bradley J. Cardinale, Marc W. Codette, and Todd Oakley, "Evolutionary History and the Effect of Biodiversity on Plant

Productivity," *Proceedings of the National Academy of Sciences* 105, no. 44 (2008): 17012–17.

3. This passage from Jacques Monod's book summarizes a worldview held by many scientists and non-scientists. "The ancient covenant is in pieces; man knows at last that he is alone in the universe's unfeeling immensity, out of which he emerged only by chance. His destiny is nowhere spelled out, nor is his duty." Jacques Monod, *Chance and Necessity; An Essay on the Natural Philosophy of Modern Biology*, 1st American ed. (New York: Knopf, 1971), 180.

4. Virginia Stem Owens, *And the Trees Clap Their Hands: Faith, Perception, and the New Physics* (Grand Rapids, Mich.: W.B. Eerdmans Pub. Co., 1983), 49.

5. Key institutions carrying on this work would include the Center for Theology and the Natural Sciences in Berkeley (http://www.ctns.org); the Zygon Center for Religion and Science in Chicago (http://www.zygoncenter.org); and the Vatican Observatory in Rome (http://www.vaticanobservatory.org); all accessed April 30, 2009.

6. In 1967 Lynn White published a widely influential paper that laid the blame on the environmental crisis at the feet of Western Christianity. See Lynn White Jr., "The Historical Roots of the Ecological Crisis," *Science* 155 (1967): 1203–1207.

7. Perhaps the most influential attack can be found in Lynn White Ibid.

8. The insight of cocreating I borrow from my mentor and good friend Philip Hefner; see his book *The Human Factor: Culture, Evolution, and Religion*, Theology and the Sciences (Minneapolis: Fortress Press, 1993).

9. This was, in fact, the subject of her presidential address to the Catholic Theological Society. Elizabeth A. Johnson, "Turn to the Heavens and the Earth: Retrieval of the Cosmos in Theology" (paper presented at the Proceedings of the Fifty-first Annual Convention of the Catholic Theological Society of America, San Diego, California, June 6–9 1996), 1.

10. Ibid., 14.

11. George Ellis, *Before the Beginning: Cosmology Explained*, ed. Peter Collins, Briefings (London; New York: Boyars/Bowerdean, 1993), 1.

12. Ibid.

13. The role of cosmology in premodern theology is well documented in Louis Bouyer, *Cosmos: The World and the Glory of God* (Petersham, Mass.: St. Bede's Publications, 1988); N. Max Wildiers, *The Theologian and His Universe: Theology and Cosmology from the Middle Ages to the Present*, ed. Paul Dunphy (New York: Seabury Press, 1982).

14. Paul Dirac, the notable physicist, once said: "It is more important to have beauty in one's equations than to have them fit experiments. It seems as though if one is working from a point of view of getting beauty in one's equations and if one has a really good insight, one is on a sure line of thought." Respected scientists recognize beauty in the universe as crucial to an understanding of the universe. Quoted in William Warthling, "Pierre Teilhard De Chardin: The Case Reopened," in *Cosmology and Theology*, ed. David Tracy and Nicholas Lash, *Concilium* (New York: Seabury Press, 1983), 70.

15. One of the meanings of the Greek word *kosmos* is "ornament." More substantially, the ancient theological consensus of a definition of beauty was unity-in-variety. For a thorough documentation on the history leading to this consensus, see Wladyslaw Tatarkiewicz, "The Great Theory of Beauty and Its Decline," *Journal of Aesthetics and Art Criticism* 31, no. 2 (1972): 165–79.

16. Claus Westermann, *A Thousand Years and a Day: Our Time in the Old Testament* (Philadelphia: Muhlenberg Press, 1962), 3, quoted in Bernhard W. Anderson, *Creation versus Chaos: The Reinterpretation of Mythical Symbolism in the Bible* (Philadelphia: Fortress Press, 1987), 82. See also Anderson's comments in *From Creation to New Creation: Old Testament Perspectives* (Minneapolis: Fortress, 1994), 104ff.

17. I give a detailed account in chapter 1 of Alejandro García-Rivera, *The Community of the Beautiful: A Theological Aesthetics* (Collegeville, Minn.: Liturgical Press, 1999).

18. See, for example, the marvelous discussion on this distinction in Amos Funkestein, *Theology and the Scientific Imagination: From the Middle Ages to the Seventeenth Century* (Princeton: Princeton University Press, 1986).

19. Stephen W. Hawking, *The Illustrated a Brief History of Time*, updated and expanded ed. (New York: Bantam Books, 1996), 232.

20. H. Paul Santmire, *The Travail of Nature: The Ambiguous Ecological Promise of Christian Theology* (Philadelphia: Fortress Press, 1985).

21. The word "ensouled" is a traditional Roman Catholic theological term referring to the relationship between body and soul. The body in Roman Catholic theology is "ensouled" and not simply a receptacle in which a soul is placed. An ensouled body is a dynamic body full of spirit. I use it here to suggest a spiritual orientation to the universe, a theme of Teilhard.

22. Elie Wiesel, "Longing for Home," in *The Longing for Home*, ed. Leroy S. Rouner (Notre Dame, Ind.: University of Notre Dame Press, 1996), 19.

23. See Douglas Farrow, *Ascension and Ecclesia: On the Significance of the Doctrine of the Ascension for Ecclesiology and Christian Cosmology* (Grand Rapids, Mich.: W.B. Eerdmans Pub., 1999), 24.

24. Jaroslav Pelikan, *Christianity and Classical Culture: The Metamorphosis of Natural Theology in the Christian Encounter with Hellenism* (New Haven: Yale University Press, 1993), 259.

25. Bouyer, *Cosmos: The World and the Glory of God*, 213.

26. See J. Jeffrey Means and Mary Ann Nelson, *Trauma and Evil: Healing the Wounded Soul* (Minneapolis, Minn: Fortress Press, 2000), Ch.1.

27. Ibid., 64–66.

28. Sue Grand, *The Reproduction of Evil: A Clinical and Cultural Perspective* (Hillsdale, N.J.: Analytic Press, 2000), 10.

29. Means and Nelson, *Trauma and Evil*, 87.

30. Ibid., 88.

31. Ibid., 93.

32. Miguel de Unamuno explored this in his powerful reflection found in Miguel de Unamuno, Anthony Kerrigan, and Martin Nozick, *The Tragic Sense of Life in Men and Nations*, Bollingen Series 85, 4 (Princeton, N.J.: Princeton University Press, 1972).

33. Burial sites going back to the dawn of human origins reveal such a sense by including items such as food, pets, utensils, etc., to be used by the dead in another life.

34. Hans Walter Wolff, *Anthropology of the Old Testament* (Philadelphia: Fortress Press, 1974), 26.

35. Ibid., 26–30.

36. Susan A. Ross, "Body," in *The New Dictionary of Catholic Spirituality*, ed. Michael Downey (Collegeville, Minn.: Liturgical Press, 1993), 93–94.

2. The Human Phenomenon: Teilhard de Chardin's New Significance

1. Quoted in "Teilhard De Chardin and His Relevance for Today," *Woodstock Report*, no. 82 (2005), http://woodstock.georgetown.edu/publications/report/r-fea82a.htm.

2. Book presentation on Cristoph Cardinal Schönborn, O.P., *Chance or Purpose? Creation, Evolution, and a Rational Faith*, trans. Henry Taylor (San Francisco: Ignatius, 2007), at Dominican School of Philosophy and Theology, February 15, 2008. The entire presentation can be viewed online at Cristoph Cardinal Schönborn, "Cardinal Schönborn, O.P. Book Presentation *Chance or Purpose?*" Dominican School of Philosophy and Theology, http://web.mac.com/sfcrews/DSPT/Link_to_Cardinal_Sch%C3%B6nborn,_O.P._Book_Presentation.html.

3. Schönborn, *Chance or Purpose?* trans. Henry Taylor (San Francisco: Ignatius Press, 2007), 141, 42.

4. N. Max Wildiers, *The Theologian and His Universe: Theology and Cosmology from the Middle Ages to the Present*, ed. Paul Dunphy (New York: Seabury Press, 1982), 190.

5. Pierre Teilhard de Chardin, *The Phenomenon of Man*, with an introduction by Sir Julian Huxley (N.Y.: Harper & Row, 1975), 31.

6. Ibid.

7. Ibid.

8. See Pieter Frans Smulders, *The Design of Teilhard De Chardin; An Essay in Theological Reflection* (Westminster, Md.: Newman Press, 1967), 27ff.

9. Quoted in Jason Scott Robert, "Molecular and Systems Biology and Bioethics," in *The Cambridge Companion to the Philosophy of Biology*, ed. David L. Hull and Michael Ruse (Cambridge; New York: Cambridge University Press, 2007), 361.

10. Stuart A. Kauffman, *At Home in the Universe: The Search for Laws of Self-Organization and Complexity* (New York: Oxford University Press, 1995), 19.

11. Ibid., 26.

12. Stuart A. Kauffman, *Reinventing the Sacred: A New View of Science, Reason and Religion* (New York: Basic Books, 2008), 3.

13. Ibid., 18.

14. Ibid., 119.

15. As of the time of this writing (October 2008), this experiment has not yet been published. Dr. Gilmour, however, has submitted his findings to a peer-review process. The above interpretation of the data, however, is mine. I do not claim that Dr. Gilmour shares such an interpretation.

16. See Smulders, *The Design of Teilhard De Chardin*, 40.

17. Pierre Teilhard de Chardin, *Activation of Energy*, trans. René Hague (San Diego: Harcourt, Inc., 1978), 280.

18. This thesis was first proposed by Alister Hardy, professor of zoology at Oxford University, in his Gifford lectures of 1963–1964, "*The Living Stream: A Restatement of Evolution Theory and Its Relation to the Spirit of Man.*" See David Hay, *Something There: The Biology of the Human Spirit* (London: Darton Longman & Todd, 2006), 39.

19. Hay, *Something There*.

20. Ibid., 130.

21. Ibid.

22. Ibid., 139.

23. Ibid., 140.

24. See Emese Nagy and Peter Molnar, "Homo Imitans or Homo Provocans? Human Imprinting Model of Neonatal Imitation," *Infant Behavior and Development* 27, no. 1 (2004): 54–63.

25. Hay, *Something There*, 141.

26. M. S. Longair and International Astronomical Union., *Confrontation of Cosmological Theories with Observational Data: Symposium No. 63 (Copernicus Symposium II) Held in Cracow, Poland, 10–12 September, 1973* (Dordrecht; Boston: D. Reidel Pub. Co., 1974), 291.

27. John D. Barrow et al., *The Anthropic Cosmological Principle*, (Oxford: Oxford University Press, 1988), 4.

28. Ibid., 5.

29. John Brockman, "The Landscape: A Talk with Leonard Susskind," *Edge: The Third Culture* (2003), http://www.edge.org/3rd_culture/susskind03/susskind_index.html.

30. A brief definition of the CDF can be found in http://www.catholic-pages.com/vatican/curia.asp. "The Congregation for the Doctrine of the Faith is the next most important dicastery of the Roman Curia. . . . This Congregation used to be called the 'Holy Office' and before that it was known as the 'Holy Roman Inquisition' (not to be confused with the Spanish Inquisition!) The primary duty

and responsibility of the Congregation for the Doctrine of the Faith is to promote and preserve the Catholic Faith throughout the Church. Anything touching on the doctrine of the faith or on morals is within the competence of this dicastery. In particular, the Congregation has the responsibility of examining the writings of theologians to ensure that they are not inconsistent with Catholic doctrine and, even, of disciplining theologians who refuse to resile from views considered erroneous or perilous to the Faith."

31. Alejandro Garcia-Rivera, "Faith and the Poor," *America*, September 17 2007: 11–13.

32. A good survey of the tradition on the cosmic Christ can be found in George A. Maloney, *The Cosmic Christ: From Paul to Teilhard* (New York: Sheed and Ward, 1968).

33. Douglas Farrow recovers the church's intense interest in the doctrine of the ascension and makes a convincing case that the doctrine is essential to understanding the church's self-identity. Douglas Farrow, *Ascension and Ecclesia: On the Significance of the Doctrine of the Ascension for Ecclesiology and Christian Cosmology* (Grand Rapids, Mich.: W.B. Eerdmans Pub., 1999).

34. Vatican II, "Sacrosanctum Concilium," in *Documents of Vatican II*, ed. Austin Flannery (Grand Rapids, Mich.: Eerdmans, 1975), Section 8.

35. Walter Brueggemann, *The Land: Place as Gift, Promise, and Challenge in Biblical Faith* (Philadelphia: Fortress Press, 1977), 187.

36. Ibid.

37. Ibid., 5.

38. Noel Roberts, *From Piltdown Man to Point Omega: The Evolutionary Theory of Teilhard De Chardin* (New York: P. Lang, 2000), 189.

39. Hans Urs von Balthasar, *Seeing the Form*, ed. Joseph Fessio and John Riches, trans. Erasmo Leiva-Merikakis, vol. 1 of *The Glory of the Lord: A Theological Aesthetics* (San Francisco: Ignatius Press, 1983), 114.

40. Pierre Teilhard de Chardin, *The Heart of Matter* (New York: Harcourt Brace Jovanovich, 1979), 64.

41. Cf. von Balthasar, *The Glory of the Lord*, 7 vols. (San Francisco: Ignatius Press, 1983–1989).

42. While many could be cited some useful books as introduction to the field include Frank Burch Brown, *Good Taste, Bad Taste, & Christian Taste: Aesthetics in Religious Life* (Oxford; New York:

Oxford University Press, 2000); Alejandro Garcia-Rivera, "On a New List of Aesthetic Categories," in *Theological Aesthetics after Hans Urs Von Balthasar*, ed. Oleg Byrchov (Oxford: Ashgate, 2008); Gesa Elsbeth Thiessen, *Theological Aesthetics: A Reader* (London: SCM Press, 2004); Richard Viladesau, *Theological Aesthetics: God in Imagination, Beauty, and Art* (New York: Oxford University Press, 1999).

43. Viladesau, *Theological Aesthetics*, 11.

44. Hans Urs von Balthasar, *Studies in Theological Style: Clerical Styles*, ed. John Kenneth Riches, trans. Brian McNeil, vol. 2 of *The Glory of the Lord: A Theological Aesthetics* (San Francisco: Ignatius Press, 1984), 173ff.

45. Excerpted from Pierre Teilhard de Chardin, *Hymn of the Universe* (New York: Harper & Row, 1965), 40–46.

My friend is dead, he who drank of life everywhere as at a sacred spring. His heart burned within him. His body lies hidden in the earth in front of Verdun. Now therefore I can repeat some of those words with which he initiated me one evening into that intense vision which gave light and peace to his life.

You want to know, he said, how the universe, in all its power and multiplicity, came to assume for me the lineaments of the face of Christ? . . . At that time . . . my mind was preoccupied with a problem partly philosophical, partly aesthetic. I was thinking: Suppose Christ should deign to appear here before me, what would he look like? How would he be dressed? Above all, in what manner, would he take his place visibly in the realm of matter and how would he stand out against the objects surrounding him? . . .

Meanwhile, my gaze had come to rest . . . on a picture representing Christ offering his heart to men. . . . As I allowed my gaze to wander over the figure's outlines I suddenly became aware that these were *melting away*: they were dissolving, but in a special manner, hard to describe in words. . . . I perceived that the vibrant atmosphere which surrounded Christ like an aureole . . . radiated outwards to infinity. Through this there passed . . . trails of phosphorescence, indicating a continuous gushing-forth to the outermost spheres of the realm of matter and delineating a sort of blood stream or nervous system running through the totality of life.

The entire universe was vibrant! And yet, when I directed my gaze to particular objects, one by one, I found them still as clearly defined as ever in their undiminished individuality. All this movement seemed to emanate from Christ, and above all his heart. . . . [Then] I saw the vision mount rapidly to its climax . . . it was the transfigured face of the Master that drew and held captive my entire attention. . . . It was the whole face that shone in this way. But the centre of the radiance and the iridescence was hidden in the transfigured portrait's eyes. Over the glorious depths of those eyes there passed in rainbow hues of reflection—unless indeed it were the creative prototype, the Idea—of everything that has power to charm us, everything that has life. . . . And the luminous simplicity of the fire which flashed from them changed, as I struggled to master it, into an inexhaustible complexity wherein were gathered all the glances that had ever warmed and mirrored back a human heart. . . .

Now while I was ardently gazing deep into the pupils of Christ's eyes . . . suddenly I beheld rising up from the depths of those same eyes what seemed like a cloud, blurring and blending all the variety I have been describing to you. Little by little, an extraordinary expression, of great intensity, spread over the diverse shades of meaning which the divine eyes revealed, first of all permeating them and then finally absorbing them all. . . . I was dumbfounded! For this final expression which had dominated and gathered up into itself all the others, was *indecipherable*. I could not tell whether it denoted an indescribable agony or a superabundance of triumphant joy. . . . In an instant my eyes were bedimmed with tears. And then, when I was once again able to look at it, the painting of Christ on the church wall had presumed once again its too precise definition and its fixity of feature.

46. Bonaventure, *The Journey of the Mind to God*, trans. Philotheus Boehner, ed. Stephen F. Brown (Indianapolis: Hackett Pub. Co., 1993).

47. Hans Urs von Balthasar, "Bonaventure," in *Studies in Theological Style: Clerical Styles*, 312ff.

48. This ancient understanding of light's formative powers is given extensive treatment in Margaret Miles, "Vision: The Eye of Body and the Eye of the Mind in St. Augustine's *De Trinitate* and the *Confessions*," *Journal of Religion* 163, no. 2 (1983): 125–42.

49. The reference to the friend is quite meaningful for it has a double reference. Teilhard indeed had a friend who was blown to pieces while he was standing next to him. Teilhard here also refers to himself. This double reference gives us a moving picture of Teilhard, who in one sense has died along with his friend at Verdun but finds life in the indecipherable beauty of the transfigured cosmic Christ.

3. Heaven and Earth

1. David Grumett, *Teilhard De Chardin: Theology, Humanity, and Cosmos*, Studies in Philosophical Theology (Leuven: Peeters, 2005), 199ff.

2. This question is also the title of one of Haught's books: John F. Haught, *Is Nature Enough? Meaning and Truth in the Age of Science* (Cambridge, UK: Cambridge University Press, 2006).

3. Russell does not explicitly use this phrase. The phrase is my summary of his eloquent appeal that science and theology need and influence each other in what he calls Creative Mutual Interaction. See Robert J. Russell, *Cosmology: From Alpha to Omega: The Creative Mutual Interaction of Theology and Science*, Theology and the Sciences (Minneapolis: Fortress Press, 2008), 4ff.

4. Carl Sagan, *Cosmos* (New York: Random House, 1980).

5. Haught, *Is Nature Enough?* 90–91.

6. Ibid., 137.

7. Russell here is quoting himself out of a presentation given at a 1986 meeting of the American Academy of Religion. Russell, *Cosmology*, 21.

8. Thomas Kuhn, *The Structure of Scientific Revolutions*, 3d ed. (Chicago: University of Chicago Press, 1996).

9. See, for example, the great study done by the noted historian of aesthetics Wladyslaw Tatarkiewicz: "The Great Theory of Beauty and Its Decline," *Journal of Aesthetics and Art Criticism* 31, no. 2 (1972): 165–79.

10. On the revelatory nature of beauty and its radical freedom, see Harold Osborne, "Revelatory Theories of Art," *The British Journal of Aesthetics* 4, no. 4 (1964).

11. The *donum/datum* structure of the universe is inspired by Henri de Lubac's well-known work, *The Mystery of the Supernatural*. It is also inspired by the notion of gift as expressed by Lewis Hyde in his insightful book, *The Gift*. Gift-language is particularly appropriate to works of art. By reframing the scholastic categories of the supernatural and natural into the categories of gift and given, I hope to bring de Lubac's insights about the nature of grace, the interlaced reality of the natural and the supernatural, into the framework of a cosmology. For the use of gift language in works of art see Lewis Hyde, *The Gift: Imagination and the Erotic Life of Property* (New York: Vintage Books, 1983). For de Lubac's classic on the nature of grace, see Henri de Lubac, *The Mystery of the Supernatural* (London: G. Chapman, 1967).

12. Actually, one could also include the passion, crucifixion, resurrection, and the last things as revealers of the *donum* nature of the cosmos but these three are especially suited.

13. This immanent rationality is a result not merely of God's absolute power, which explains creation *ex nihilo*, but more importantly a result of God's ordaining power. Thomas F. Torrance, *Space, Time and Incarnation* (Oxford: Oxford University Press, 1969), 67–68.

14. Ibid., 74ff.

15. Torrance, *Space, Time, and Resurrection* (Grand Rapids: Eerdmans, 1976), 129.

16. I wish not to be misunderstood here. I am not insisting that science *per se* take into account the *donum* character of the cosmos. I am insisting, however, that a theological cosmology must include the gift nature of the cosmos as it interprets scientific discovery based on the given-ness of the cosmos.

17. John Polkinghorne, *The God of Hope and the End of the World* (New Haven, Conn.: Yale University Press, 2003), xxiii.

18. The proceedings of that three-year project sponsored by the Center of Theological Inquiry at Princeton were published as a

volume: J. C. Polkinghorne and Michael Welker, *The End of the World and the Ends of God: Science and Theology on Eschatology*, Theology for the Twenty-First Century (Harrisburg, Pa.: Trinity Press International, 2000).

19. Ibid., 295.

20. Andrew T. Lincoln, *Paradise Now and Not Yet: Studies in the Role of the Heavenly Dimension in Paul's Thought with Special Reference to His Eschatology* (Cambridge: Cambridge University Press, 1981), 115.

21. Ibid., 140–41.

22. Ibid., 185.

23. Tim Cresswell, *Place: A Short Introduction* (Malden, Mass.: Blackwell Publications, 2004), 50–51.

24. Edward S. Casey, *The Fate of Place: A Philosophical History* (Berkeley: University of California Press, 1997), ix.

25. John Inge, *A Christian Theology of Place*, Explorations in Practical, Pastoral, and Empirical Theology (Aldershot, England: Ashgate, 2003), 4.

26. Torrance, *Space, Time and Incarnation*, 4.

27. Ibid., 4–5. See also Casey, *The Fate of Place*, 23ff.

28. Torrance, *Space, Time and Incarnation*, 7. Also see, Casey, *The Fate of Place*, 50ff.

29. Torrance, *Space, Time and Incarnation*, 22ff.

30. Ibid., 12.

31. Casey, *The Fate of Place*, 75ff.

32. Quoted in Inge, *A Christian Theology of Place*, 6.

33. Edward S. Casey, *Getting Back into Place: Toward a Renewed Understanding of the Place-World* (Bloomington: Indiana University Press, 1993), 6ff.

34. Gaston Bachelard, M. Jolas, and John R. Stilgoe, *The Poetics of Space* (Boston: Beacon, 1994), xvi.

35. Ibid., xviii.

36. Ibid., 4.

37. Ibid., 183ff.

38. Ibid., 202.

39. Ibid., 203.

40. Grumett, *Teilhard De Chardin*, 139.

41. Pierre Teilhard De Chardin, *The Human Phenomenon* (Brighton: Sussex Academic Press, 2003), 3; quoted in Grumett, *Teilhard De Chardin*, 139.

42. David Grumett, *Christ in the World of Matter: Teilhard De Chardin's Religious Experience and Vision*, vol. 45, 2nd Series Occasional Paper (Lampeter, Wales: Religious Experience Research Center, University of Wales, 2006), 5ff.

43. Louis M. Savary, *Teilhard De Chardin, the Divine Milieu Explained: A Spirituality for the 21st Century* (New York: Paulist Press, 2007), 170.

44. Grumett, *Teilhard De Chardin*, 228.

45. Edmund Hill in his book *Being Human* summarizes a great deal of Roman Catholic anthropology by exposing the Priestly and Yahwist views in Genesis as an account of attitudes of these writers toward the city and the garden. In this respect, the Tower of Babel signifies the Yahwist's pessimistic attitude toward the city as humanity's true home. The Priestly writer, on the other hand, has an entirely opposite attitude toward the city. Hill also sees this difference in attitude as running through the entire Scriptures. Thus, Hill sees Roman Catholic anthropology as addressing a tension between the garden as humanity's true home or the city as humanity's true destiny. I agree with his assessment and use his insight to develop this section. For a fuller account see Edmund Hill, *Being Human: A Biblical Perspective* (London: G. Chapman, 1984).

46. Michael Crichton and Chip Kidd, *Jurassic Park: A Novel* (New York: Knopf, 1990), 306–7.

47. I believe there is an inextricable connection between commodified technology and modern science. I do not intend to demonstrate this point here; but it is a point that seems to be self-evident or, if not, a point that can be easily argued.

48. Philip J. Hefner, *Technology and Human Becoming* (Minneapolis: Fortress, 2003), 44.

49. Mihaly Csikszentmihaly, "Consciousness for the Twenty-First Century," *Zygon* 26, no. 1 (1991): 4.; quoted in Hefner, *Technology and Human Becoming*, 52.

50. Hefner, *Technology and Human Becoming*, 55.

51. Hyde, *The Gift*, xi.

52. Ibid., xii.

53. Ibid., 48.

4. Endless Forms Most Beautiful

1. This section, though altered, is substantially the material found in Alejandro Garcia-Rivera, "Endless Forms Most Beautiful," *Theology and Science* 5, no. 2 (2007): 125–35.

2. Quoted in Sean B. Carroll, *Endless Forms Most Beautiful: The New Science of Evo Devo and the Making of the Animal Kingdom*, (New York: W.W. Norton, 2005), 281–82.

3. By *telos* I mean the *telos* of a design. A chair, for example, is the end product or *telos* of an artisan's work. I am not arguing, however, for a view of natural form as direct intervention by divine design. I am pointing out that nature herself appears to design as an artist or artisan designs. *Mindfulness* refers not to divine intelligence intervening in natural process but that intelligence is ubiquitous in nature.

4. *Form* is a term with a long history and claimed by various disciplines, philosophy, art, science and many others. The historian of aesthetic ideas Wladyslaw Tatarkiewicz has distilled the history of form into a finite set of basic categories. There are five basic definitions of form: *Form A*: arrangement of parts; the form of a portico is the arrangement of its columns; the form of a melody is the order of its sounds. *Form B*: what is directly given to the senses; the sound of words in poetry is its form. *Form C*: the boundary or contour of an object. *Form D* (substantial form): the conceptual essence of an object (entelechy). *Form E*: the contribution of the mind to the perceived object (Kant). While any of these meanings can be used when referring to form, I will concentrate on what Tatarkiewicz calls Form D, substantial form. I argue that substantial form is the relevant meaning when referring to natural, beautiful forms. I will also argue that this meaning itself has to be expanded to include a dynamic dimension intrinsic to living forms. The history of these meanings can be found in Wladyslaw Tatarkiewicz, "Form: History of One Term and Five Concepts," in *A History of Six Ideas: An Essay in Aesthetics*, Melbourne International Philosophy Series, vol. 5 (The Hague: Nijhoff, 1980), 220–43.

5. Ernst Mayr proposed that living nature has intrinsic telic dimensions that do not destroy the autonomy or integrity of natural process. He called these *teleomatic*, processes that exhibit goal-directedness according to laws of nature such as a particle seeking a lower potential,

and *teleonomic*, processes whose goal-directedness is part of a natural program, such as the development of an individual from a fertilized zygote. His specific argument can be found in Ernst Mayr, "Teleological and Teleonomic: A New Analysis," *Boston Studies in the Philosophy of Science* 14 (1974). A more expansive and mature argument is exposed in *idem, The Growth of Biological Thought: Diversity, Evolution, and Inheritance* (Cambridge, Mass.: Belknap Press, 1982).

6. Eric Schneider was at that time director of the National Marine Water Quality Laboratory of the Environmental Protection Agency (EPA).

7. Eric D. Schneider and Dorion Sagan, *Into the Cool: Energy Flow, Thermodynamics, and Life* (Chicago: University of Chicago Press, 2005), 320–21.

8. A gradient might be thought of as a natural analogy to what theologians call *kenosis*. *Kenosis* is a term used in theology to describe the self-emptying nature of God, such as in the trinitarian processions and the incarnation. Here I am using it in an analogous way to describe the dynamism of open systems. Open systems exist because they empty their energy into the "cool," that is, the heat death of entropy. A gradient, then, could be seen as the continuous self-emptying of energy from the interior to the exterior of an open system. As open, dynamic systems, they are not only self-emptying but also give rise to beautiful, living forms.

9. Schneider and Sagan, *Into the Cool*, 121.

10. Beauty in nature is perhaps the most problematic of aesthetic issues. The proposal that such natural beauty exists is hampered by the uncritical belief that "beauty is in the eye of the beholder." Whitehead addressed this uncritical belief by a parody of common scientific opinion of natural beauty. "Nature gets credit which should in truth be reserved for ourselves: the rose for its scent: the nightingale for his song: the sun for his radiance. The poets are entirely mistaken. They should address their lyrics to themselves, and should turn them into odes of self-congratulation on the excellency of the human mind. Nature is a dull affair, soundless, scentless, colourless; merely the hurrying of material, endlessly, meaninglessly." Alfred North Whitehead, *Science and the Modern World* (New York: Free Press, 1925), 80. I suppose one cannot convince by rational argument that natural beauty truly and really exists, but I cannot imagine any genuine theology, indeed any spirituality, maintaining that natural beauty is to be found

merely and solely in the human emotional response to natural reality. Nonetheless, the reader should be aware that it is quite difficult to "prove" that nature possesses an intrinsic beauty. See, for example, Alejandro Garcia-Rivera, Mark Graves, and Carl Neuman, "Beauty in the Living World," *Zygon* 44 (2009): 243–64.

11. Carroll, *Endless Forms Most Beautiful*, 7.

12. This point is insightfully brought out by Herbert Scheit, "Hylemorphism," in *Sacramentum Mundi: An Encyclopedia of Theology*, ed. Karl Rahner (London: Burns & Oates, 1968), 82–84.

13. See Robert Rosen, "Essays on Life Itself," in *Complexity in Ecological Systems series* (New York: Columbia University Press, 2000), 148ff.

14. See Michael Dodds, O.P., "Top Down, Bottom Up or Inside Out? Retrieving Aristotelian Causality in Contemporary Science," in *Science, Philosophy, and Theology*, ed. John O'Callaghan (South Bend, Ind.: St. Augustine's Press, 2006).

15. No doubt many may see at this point the specter of vitalism rising out of the notion of living form. *Vitalism* refers to the view that organisms cannot be solely understood in terms of physico-chemical factors but in terms of an independent vital principle or force. This is neither my intention nor my belief. Nonetheless, I do believe life is a real phenomenon and not an epiphenomenon of either Newtonian or quantum-mechanical forces. To assert the natural reality of living forms does not necessarily mean I am espousing an additional principle to physical or chemical causes. I am, however, espousing an expansion of our physical understanding of the universe to include formal causes. And then, I am espousing not simply Aristotle's version of formal causality but dynamic formal causality as suggested by nature herself. I do not see this as proposing vitalistic dualism. It is, however, a challenge to a purely monistic view of natural reality. As I have argued earlier, the cosmos must be understood in neither monistic or dualistic terms. Reality is more complex than either of these alternatives would suggest. In any case, to the reader who is interested in reading deeper about vitalism I can recommend the dated but still valuable volume by Hans Driesch: *The History and Theory of Vitalism* (London: Macmillan, 1914).

16. The reader here may note that this gives living form a dramatic, narrative structure. I do not develop this aspect of living form in this book, but I believe there is a dramatic structure to evolution that needs to be developed further. I hope to do so in another book.

17. Quoted in Carroll, *Endless Forms Most Beautiful*, 284.

18. Ibid., 11.

19. Ibid., 294.

20. David Kohn, "The Aesthetic Construction of Darwin's Theory," in *The Elusive Synthesis: Aesthetics and Science*, ed. Alfred I. Tauber (Boston: Kluwer, 1996), 13.

21. Charles Darwin, *The Origin of Species*, quoted in Carroll, *Endless Forms Most Beautiful*, 489.

22. This description of beauty is the conclusion from a well-known work by the great aesthetician Wladyslaw Tatarkiewicz; cf. his "The Great Theory of Beauty and Its Decline," *Journal of Aesthetics and Art Criticism* 31, no. 2 (1972): 165–79.

23. Patrick Sherry, *Spirit and Beauty: An Introduction to Theological Aesthetics*, 2nd ed. (London: SCM, 2002), 84.

24. Bonaventure ed. Ewert H. Cousins, *Bonaventure* (New York: Paulist Press, 1978), 72–74. These pages correspond to Bonaventure's *Itinerarium*, chap. 2, 7–9.

25. Sherry, *Spirit and Beauty*, 97.

26. Hans Urs von Balthasar, *Seeing the Form*, ed. Joseph Fessio and John Riches, trans. Erasmo Leiva-Merikakis, vol. 1 of *The Glory of the Lord: A Theological Aesthetics* (San Francisco: Ignatius Press, 1983), 150.

27. Ibid., 151.

28. Ibid., 494.

29. Ibid., 247.

30. In general, it means God's redemptive call for the human creature to live within the divine life. Particularly, the supernatural refers to the scholastic distinction between the natural order and the supernatural order. The natural order refers to what the universe can account properly for itself in the nature of all existing creatures. In the case of the human creature, it is human nature without the benefit of God's grace. The supernatural, on the other hand, refers to that which cannot be accounted for by mere self-referential nature. In terms of human nature, it is the sphere of grace and gift that elevates human nature to a new level of existence. Much controversy has taken place over this distinction. See, for example, Eulalio R. Baltazar, *Teilhard and the Supernatural* (Baltimore: Helicon, 1966); Henri de Lubac, *The Mystery of the Supernatural* (New York: Crossroad, 1998).

31. C.I.C. 1166, quoted in Patrick Bishop, S.J., "Sacramentals," in *The New Dictionary of Sacramental Worship*, ed. Peter E. Fink (Collegeville, Minn.: Liturgical Press, 1990), 1114.

32. Vatican II, "Sacrosanctum Concilium," in *Documents of Vatican II*, ed. Austin Flannery (Grand Rapids, Mich.: Eerdmans, 1975), Section 61.

33. See, for example, Thomas F. Mathews, *The Clash of Gods: A Reinterpretation of Early Christian Art* (Princeton, N.J.: Princeton University Press, 1993), 92ff.

5. The Garden of God: Toward a Theological Cosmology

1. The poem is called "As Kingfishers Catch Fire"

As kingfishers catch fire, dragonflies draw flame;
> As tumbled over rim in roundy wells
> Stones ring; like each tucked string tells, each hung bell's
Bow swung finds tongue to fling out broad its name;
Each mortal thing does one thing and the same:
> Deals out that being indoors each one dwells;
> Selves—goes itself; myself it speaks and spells,
Crying What I do is me: for that I came.

Found in Gerard Manley Hopkins, ed. Robert Seymour Bridges, *Poems of Gerard Manley Hopkins Now First Published* (London: H. Milford, 1918).

2. Virginia Stem Owens, *And the Trees Clap Their Hands: Faith, Perception, and the New Physics* (Grand Rapids, Mich.: W.B. Eerdmans Pub. Co., 1983), 44.

3. Gustavo Gutiérrez, *On Job: God-Talk and the Suffering of the Innocent* (Maryknoll, N.Y.: Orbis Books, 1987), 13.

4. Leon Jaroff, "Window on the Stone Age," *Time*, January 30 1995, http://www.time.com/time/magazine/article/0,9171,982386,00.html, accessed May 7, 2009.

5. Ian Tattersall, *Becoming Human: Evolution and Human Uniqueness* (New York: Harcourt Brace, 1998), 3.

6. Wentzel Van Huyssteen, *Alone in the World? Human Uniqueness in Science and Theology* (Grand Rapids, Mich.: William B. Eerdmans, 2006), 170.

7. See in particular Margaret Wright Conkey and Olga Soffer, "Studying Ancient Visual Cultures," in *Beyond Art: Pleistocene Image and Symbol*, ed. Margaret Wright Conkey, Nina G. Jablonski. Wattis Symposium Series in Anthropology (San Francisco: California Academy of Sciences, 1997), 1–16.

8. Van Huyssteen, *Alone in the World?* 175.

9. J. David Lewis-Williams, *The Mind in the Cave: Consciousness and the Origins of Art* (London: Thames & Hudson, 2002), 73.

10. Nicholas Wolterstorff, "Beyond Beauty and the Aesthetic in the Engagement of Religion and Art," in *Theological Aesthetics after Hans Urs Von Balthasar*, ed. Oleg Byrchov (Aldershot, Eng.: Ashgate, 2008), 119–33.

11. John Dewey, *Art as Experience* (New York: Capricorn Books, 1959).

12. See Alejandro Garcia-Rivera, "On a New List of Aesthetic Categories," in *Theological Aesthetics after Hans Urs Von Balthasar*.

13. Quoted in David E. Cooper, *A Philosophy of Gardens* (Oxford: Clarendon Press, 2006), 146.

14. Tattersall, *Becoming Human*, 78.

15. Cooper argues that the garden is "a place peculiarly suited to the conduct of philosophical thought and discussion" to be "apprehended with a mysterious sense that [its] components deeply matter to us." Cooper, *A Philosophy of Gardens*, 6.

16. Ibid., 10.

17. Ibid., 20.

18. Robin Matthews, "In the Trail of the Serpent: A Theological Perspective," in *The Meaning of Gardens: Idea, Place, and Action*, ed. Mark Francis and Randolph T. Hester (Cambridge, Mass.: MIT Press, 1990), 46.

19. Teilhard's evolutionary view is inspired more by Lamarck than by Darwin. Yet it would be simplistic to merely label Teilhard a Lamarckian. Perhaps it would be more accurate to say that Teilhard saw creativity as part of the evolutionary process. A good understanding of Teilhard's evolutionary views can be found in David Grumett,

Teilhard De Chardin: Theology, Humanity, and Cosmos, Studies in Philosophical Theology (Leuven: Peeters, 2005), 197–237.

20. Pope John Paul II in his "Letter to the Artists" sees God's image revealed in the creativity of the artist. Thus, human dignity based on the image of God is now also seen as based on human creativity. Pope John Paul II, "Letter to Artists," *Origins* 28, no. 46 (1999).

21. In this, I follow, in part, Irenaeus's belief that human suffering is due to our first parent's child-like innocence and helps us learn how to become ever more human. I myself believe the fall is more serious than Irenaeus would have us believe; yet I agree with him that humans are developing or, in my view, evolving toward their full potential as humans. My account of human evolution, however, would be more in line with Teilhard's. A good introduction to Irenaeus's thought can be found in Mary Ann Donovan, *One Right Reading? A Guide to Irenaeus* (Collegeville, Minn.: Liturgical Press, 1997).

22. Carolyn Merchant, *Reinventing Eden: The Fate of Nature in Western Culture* (New York: Routledge, 2003), 2.

23. Ibid.

24. I take much of this thesis from Borgmann's excellent analysis of postmodern technology. See Albert Borgmann, *Power Failure: Christianity in the Culture of Technology* (Grand Rapids, Mich.: Brazos Press, 2003).

25. Carolyn Merchant sees these two temptations quite clearly in our approaches to Eden today. Merchant, *Reinventing Eden*.

26. Christopher Alexander and Center for Environmental Structure, *The Phenomenon of Life*, vol. 1: *The Nature of Order* (Berkeley, Calif.: Center for Environmental Structure, 2002), 85–86.

27. If theodicy is theology's attempt to justify the goodness and power of God in light of evil, then anthropodicy is the attempt to justify the goodness and dignity of the human in light of the evil humans do. I believe that anthropodicy has become more crucial for theology in the twenty-first century.

Index

Form in flux, 84, 109–110
Frailty of the flesh, xii, 19, 21, 118, 122–23, 125–27, 130–32
Future, xii, 4, 6, 9, 14–15, 25, 44–45, 50–51, 70, 104–106, 127, 131–32

Galileo, 30, 69
Genesis, 74, 75, 111, 113, 145n.45
Gift, 58–61, 64, 77–80, 89, 91, 99–100, 102–103, 118, 124–25, 127,
    129, 132, 143n.11, 143n.16, 149n.30
Gilmour, Darren, 32
Gnostics, 20
God's absolute power, 11–12, 68–70, 143n.13
God's ordaining power, 11, 68–69, 98, 143n.13
Grace, 60, 64–65, 75, 99–100, 121, 125, 143n.11, 149n.30
Grand Modern Narrative of Art, 116-7, 119
Grand, Sue, 18
Graves, Mark, 32
Greek cosmology, 63

Haught, John, 54ff, 142n.2
Hawking, Stephen, 12
Hay, David, 34–35
Hebrew cosmology, 63ff
Hefner, Phillip, 77, 80, 134n.8
Holy Spirit, xii, 22, 28, 43–45, 51–52, 64, 94–95, 97–99, 101–102, 109
Hopkins, Gerard Manley, 50, 81, 108, 150n.1
Human evolution, 101, 113ff, 152n.21
Human freedom, 44–45, 77
Hyde, Lewis, 78, 143n.11

Incarnation, 21, 59, 61, 66, 147n.8
In-formed, 98–99
Integrity of God, 112–13, 131
Interiority, 27, 29–30, 32, 70, 73, 106, 123
Interlacing, ix–xii, 9, 15
Intimate immensity, 71–72, 74, 105

Job, 17, 111–113
Johnson, Elizabeth, 6
Jurassic Park, 76, 80

LaVergne, TN USA
30 May 2010
184328LV00004B/6/P